Early Praise for *In the Line of Fire*

"In my role at Cisco Systems, I am confronted with challenging questions from customers, government leaders, press, and analysts on a daily basis. The techniques used in this book, *In the Line of Fire*, are spot on; providing straightforward ways to be on the offense in all communications situations."

Sue Bostrom, SVP Internet Business Solutions Group and Worldwide Government Affairs, Cisco Systems

"In an era where businesspeople and politicians unfortunately have proven their inability to be honest with bad news, I believe this book should be prescribed reading in every business school, and for every management training session. In fact, I hope it is read by a far wider audience than that. It's just what our society needs right now."

Po Bronson, author of the bestselling *What Should I Do With My Life?*

"Jerry Weissman tells the tales of the makings of presidents and kings, the dramas of the dramatic moments of our time, and in each episode he uncovers the simple truths behind what makes great leaders like Ronald Reagan and Colin Powell loved and trusted. Great truths made simple and compelling for any leader to use."

Scott Cook, Founding CEO, Intuit

"Jerry's book is a must-read for any presenter facing tough and challenging questions from their audience. This book provides the fundamental foundation on how to prepare, be agile, and take charge no matter how difficult the question."

Leslie Culbertson, Corporate Vice President Director of Corporate Finance, Intel Corporation

"During one of the most important periods of my career, Jerry used the concepts in *In the Line of Fire* to prepare me and my team for the EarthLink IPO road show. He helped us field tough questions from the toughest possible audience: potential investors, but the same skills are necessary for every audience.

Sky Dayton, Founder EarthLink and Boingo Wireless, CEO SK-EarthLink

"Jerry Weissman helped prepare my management team for our recent IPO. I sat in on some of the sessions and was most impressed with Jerry's innovative ways of teaching and optimizing effective executive communication methods. This training, encapsulated well in his new book, *In the Line of Fire*," paid off handsomely during our numerous road show presentations."

Ray Dolby, Founder and Chairman, Dolby Laboratories, Inc.

"Whether you're a classroom teacher or the President, this book will help you be an effective communicator. This book is so insightful, reading it feels like cheating. Tough questions no longer test my limits."

Reed Hastings, Founder and CEO, Netflix

"Even the greatest start encounters tough questions. Read Jerry's book before you need it, or you'll be in deep sushi."

Guy Kawasaki, author of the bestselling *The Art of the Start*

"Have you ever been faced with a tough question? Jerry Weissman shows how it's not necessarily what the answer is. It's how you answer that will allow you to prevail and win!"

Tim Koogle, Founding CEO, Yahoo!

"Jerry's technique is both masterful and universal because it finds common ground between audience and speaker, hard questions and direct answers, all with a very simple principle: truth."

Pierre Omidyar, Founder of eBay and Omidyar Network

"I've been asking tough questions for half a century and listening to variously brilliant, boring, evasive or illuminating answers. Jerry Weissman's book will help anyone...anyone...answer even the toughest questions."

Mike Wallace, Senior Correspondent, *Sixty Minutes*, CBS News

In the Line of Fire

How to Handle Tough Questions ...When It Counts

In the Line of Fire

How to Handle Tough Questions ...When It Counts

Jerry Weissman

Author of
Presenting to Win: The Art of Telling Your Story

An Imprint of Pearson Education
Upper Saddle River, NJ • New York • London • San Francisco • Toronto • Sydney •
Tokyo • Singapore • Hong Kong • Cape Town • Madrid
Paris • Milan • Munich • Amsterdam

Library of Congress Catalog Number: 2005922492

Vice President and Editor-in-Chief: *Tim Moore*
Acquisitions Editor: *Paula Sinnott*
Editorial Assistant: *Kate E. Stephenson*
Development Editor: *Russ Hall*
International Marketing Manager: *Tim Galligan*
Cover Designer: *Sandra Schroeder*
Managing Editor: *Gina Kanouse*
Senior Project Editor: *Lori Lyons*
Copy Editor: *Christal Andry*
Senior Indexer: *Cheryl Lenser*
Senior Compositor: *Gloria Schurick*
Art Consultant: *Nichole Nears*
Video Consultant: *Jennifer Turcotte*
Manufacturing Buyer: *Dan Uhrig*

Publishing as Prentice Hall
Upper Saddle River, New Jersey 07458

Prentice Hall offers excellent discounts on this book when ordered in quantity for bulk purchases or special sales. For more information, please contact U.S. Corporate and Government Sales, 1-800-382-3419, corpsales@pearsontechgroup.com. For sales outside the U.S., please contact International Sales, 1-317-581-3793, international@pearsontechgroup.com.

Printed in the United States of America

First Printing: June 2005

ISBN 0-13-185517-4

Pearson Education LTD.
Pearson Education Australia PTY, Limited.
Pearson Education Singapore, Pte. Ltd.
Pearson Education North Asia, Ltd.
Pearson Education Canada, Ltd.
Pearson Educatio[ac]n de Mexico, S.A. de C.V.
Pearson Education—Japan
Pearson Education Malaysia, Pte. Ltd.

For Lucie...at last.

CONTENTS

About the Author

Jerry Weissman, the world's #1 corporate presentations coach, founded and leads Power Presentations, Ltd. in Foster City, CA. His private clients include executives at hundreds of the world's top companies, including Yahoo!, Intel, Cisco Systems, Intuit, Dolby Laboratories, and Microsoft.

Weissman coached Cisco's executives before their immensely successful IPO roadshow; afterward, the firm's chairman attributed at least two to three dollars of Cisco's offering price to his work. Since then, he has prepared executives for nearly 500 IPO roadshows, helping them raise hundreds of billions of dollars.

Weissman is author of the global best-seller *Presenting to Win: The Art of Telling Your Story* (Financial Times Prentice Hall, 2003).

INTRODUCTION

Agility Versus Force

During my 40 years in the communications trade ranging from the control rooms of the CBS Broadcast Center in Manhattan to the boardrooms of some of America's most prestigious corporations, I have heard...*and* have asked...some highly challenging questions. One of the most challenging I ever heard came during Bill Clinton's presidency when he was engulfed in the firestorm ignited by the revelation of his extramarital affair with Monica Lewinsky, a White House intern.

Despite intense public and media pressure, Clinton continued to fulfill his presidential obligations, among them hosting a state visit by the Prime Minister of the United Kingdom, Tony Blair. On the afternoon of February 6, 1998, after the two heads of state made their customary prepared statements to the press, President Clinton opened the floor to questions from an audience packed with reporters. At that point, he became fair game for nonstate questions on the subject that was uppermost in the minds of the media and the public. One question in particular came from Wolf Blitzer, the senior CNN political correspondent:

> *Mr. President, Monica Lewinsky's life has been changed forever, her family's life has been changed forever. I wonder how you feel about that and what, if anything, you'd like to say to Monica Lewinsky at this minute?*

The stinging question brought a few scattered titters from the other reporters. Looking straight ahead, right at Blitzer, Clinton smiled and bit his lower lip, an expression that had become his trademark (see Figure I.1).

▲ **FIGURE I.1** *Bill Clinton reacts to a question about Monica Lewinsky.*

Then he said,

> *That's good!*

The crowded room erupted in laughter. After it subsided, Clinton continued:

> *That's good...but at this minute, I am going to stick with my position and not comment. [I.1]*

Blitzer had nailed the acknowledged charismatic master of communication skills at his own game, and the master acknowledged it publicly for all to hear. Fortunately for Clinton, he was able to default to his legal situation and not answer.

Very few people on the face of this planet have the expertise, the charm, the quickness of wit, or the legal circumstances to respond so deftly to challenging questions. Yet very few people on the face of this planet sail through life without being confronted with tough questions. The purpose of this book and its many real-life examples is to provide you with the skills to handle such questions, and *only* such questions. If all the questions you are ever faced with were of the "Where do I sign?" variety, you could spend your time with a good mystery novel instead. Forewarned is forearmed.

One other forewarning: All the techniques you are about to learn require absolute truth. The operative word in the paragraph above, as well as on the cover of this book, is "handle," meaning how to deal with tough questions. While providing an answer is an integral part of that "handling," every answer you give to every question you get must be honest and straightforward. If not, all the other techniques will be for naught. With a truthful answer as your foundation, all those techniques will enable you to survive, if not prevail, in the line of fire.

Challenging Questions

We begin our journey of discovery by understanding why people ask challenging questions. Journalists such as Wolf Blitzer ask these kinds of questions because, being familiar with the classical art of drama, they know that conflict creates drama. *Aristotle 101.*

Why do people in business ask challenging questions? Because they are mean-spirited? Perhaps. Because they want to test your mettle? Perhaps. More likely it is because when you are presenting your case, which is *just* the case in almost every decisive communication in business...as well as in *all* walks of life...you are asking your opposite party or parties, your target audience, to change. Most human beings are resistant to change, and so they kick the tires. *You* are the tires.

In the most mission-critical of all business presentations, the Initial Public Offering (IPO) road show...a form of communication I have had the opportunity and privilege to influence with nearly 500 companies, among them Cisco Systems, Intuit, Yahoo!, and Dolby Laboratories...presenters ask their investor audiences to change: to buy a stock that never existed. In fact, when companies offer shares to the public for the first time, the U.S. Securities and Exchange Commission mandates that the companies specifically state their intentions in print. The SEC requires distribution of a prospectus containing a boilerplate sentence that reads, "There has been no prior public market for the company's common stock." In other words, "Invest at your own risk." *Caveat emptor.* As a result, when the companies' executive teams take their presentations on the road, they are inevitably assaulted with challenging questions from their potential investors.

While the stakes in an IPO road show are exceedingly high...in the tens of millions of dollars...the character of the challenge is no different from that of potential customers considering a new product, potential partners considering a strategic relationship, pressured managers considering a request for additional expenditures, concerned citizens considering a dark horse candidate, or even affluent contributors considering a donation to a nascent, not-for-profit cause.

The inherent challenge in these circumstances is compounded in presentation settings where the intensity level is raised by several additional factors:

- **Public exposure.** The risk of a mistake is magnified in large groups.
- **Group dynamics.** The more people in the audience, the more difficult it is to maintain control.
- **One against many.** Audiences have an affinity bond among themselves and apart from the presenter or speaker.

The result is open season on the lone figure spotlighted at the front of the room, who then becomes fair game for a volley of even more challenging questions.

How, then, to level the playing field? How, then, to give the presenter the weapons to withstand the attack? How, then, to survive the *slings and arrows* unleashed in the form of questions?

The answer lies in the David versus Goliath match, in which a mere youth was able to defeat a mighty giant using only a stone from a slingshot. This biblical parable has numerous equivalents in military warfare. History abounds with examples in which small, outnumbered, under-equipped units were able to combat vastly superior forces by using adroit maneuvers and clever defenses. Remember the Alamo, but also remember Thermopylae, Masada, Agincourt, The Bastille, Stalingrad, The Battle of the Bulge, Iwo Jima, and The Six-Day War. All these legendary battles share one common denominator: leverage, or the use of *agility to counter force.*

Use agility to counter force.

Martial Arts

For our purposes, the most pertinent modern equivalent is the martial arts, in which a skilled practitioner can compete with a superior opponent by using dexterity rather than might. Bruce Lee, a diminutive kick boxer, became an international star by virtue of his uncanny ability to prevail over multiple and mightier *armed* opponents using *only* his flying feet and hands. Evolved from Asian philosophy and religion, the martial arts employ these critical mental and physical skills:

- Concentration
- Self-defense

- Balance
- Agility
- Discipline
- Self-control

A solitary presenter or speaker facing challenging questions from a hostile audience can deploy these same pivotal dynamics *against a sea of troubles and, by opposing, end them.* This book will translate each of these martial arts skills into Q&A techniques and then demonstrate how you can apply them in your mission-critical encounters. The objective is to put you in charge of those sessions and enable you to win in your exchanges when it counts.

This objective can be stated in one word, although it will take 168 pages to present them in full. That one word is *control.* When you are confronted with tough questions, you can control

- The question
- Your answer
- The questioner
- The audience
- The time
- Yourself

Effective Management *Perceived*

A synonym for the verb "control" is "manage." Therefore, the subliminal perception of a well-handled question is *Effective Management.* Of course, no one in your target audience is going to conclude that because you fielded a tough question well, you are a good manager. That is a bit of a stretch. But the converse proves the point. If your response to a challenging question is defensive, evasive, or contentious, you lose credibility…and with it the likelihood of attaining your objective in the interchange.

If your response is prompt, assured, and to the point, you will be far more likely to emerge unscathed, if not fully victorious.

This concept goes all the way back to the first millennium. In *Beowulf*, the heroic saga that is one of the foundation works of the English language, one of the lines reads: "Behavior that's admired is the path to power among people everywhere." [I.2]

In the twenty-first century, that same concept as it relates to tough questions was expressed by David Bellet, the Chairman of Crown Advisors International, one of Wall Street's most successful long-term investment firms. Having been an early backer of many successful companies, among them Hewlett-Packard, Sony, and Intel, David is solicited to invest almost daily. In response, he often fires challenging questions at his petitioners.

"When I ask questions," says David, "I don't really have to have the full answer because I can't know the subject as well as the presenter. What I look for is whether the presenter has thought about the question, been candid, thorough, and direct and how the presenter handles himself or herself under stress; if that person has the passion of 'fire in the belly' and can stand tall in the line of fire."

Baptism Under Fire

I, too, was once in the business of asking tough questions. Before becoming a presentation coach for those nearly 500 IPO road shows, as well as for thousands of other presentations ranging from raising private capital to launching products, seeking partnerships, and requisitioning budget approvals, I spent a decade as a news and public affairs producer at CBS Television in New York. As a student of the classical art of drama and with the full knowledge that conflict creates drama, I became an expert at asking challenging questions.

My baptism under fire came early in my tenure at CBS. In 1963, I was assigned to be the Associate Producer of a documentary series called *Eye on New York*, whose host was the then newly hired Mike Wallace. Although *Sixty Minutes,* Mike's magnum opus, would not debut for another five years, he came to CBS largely on the strength of the reputation he had developed on another New York television station as an aggressive interrogator on a series called *Night Beat.* Mike had regularly bombarded his *Night Beat* guests with tough questions and was intent on maintaining his inquisitorial reputation at CBS. He fully expected his Associate Producer to provide him with live ammunition for his firepower. Heaven help me when I did not.

Fortunately, I survived Mike's slings and arrows by learning how to devise tough questions. In the process, I also learned how to handle those same questions. This book is a compilation of those techniques, seasoned and battle-tested for nearly 20 years in business with my corporate clients.

You will find the techniques illustrated with a host of examples from the business world, as well as from the white-hot cauldron of debate in the political world.* In that world...unlike business and other areas of persuasive endeavor where facts and logic are at stake...the issue is a contest of individuals pitted one against the other in mortal combat: Only the winner survives. Although the lone presenter or speaker pitted against the challenging forces of an audience is not quite as lethal as politics, the one-against-many odds raise the stakes. Therefore, analyzing the dynamics of political debate will serve as a tried and tested role model for your Q&A skills. The following pages will provide you with an arsenal of weapons you will need when you step into the line of fire.

Expanding upon David Bellet's observation, the objective of this book is not so much to show you how to respond with the right answers as it is to show you how to establish a positive perception with your audiences by giving them the confidence that you can manage adversity, stay the course, and stay in *control.*

*For a companion DVD of the original videos of these examples, please visit www.powerltd.com.

The Critical Dynamics of Q&A

To fully appreciate the importance of control in handling tough questions, we should first look at the consequences of loss of control. A vivid example of such a disastrous unraveling comes from an episode of the 1970s comedy television series, *The Bob Newhart Show*. The widely known series is still running in syndication. One particular episode has become a classic. In it, Newhart plays a psychologist named Robert Hartley, who amiably agrees to appear on a Chicago television program to be interviewed by Ruth Corley, the program's hostess. This is the interview:

Ruth Corley: *Good morning, Dr. Hartley. Thank you for coming. I hope it's not too early for you.*

Dr. Hartley: *No, I had to get up to be on television.*

Ruth Corley: *Well, I'm glad you're relaxed. I'm a little nervous myself, I mean, I've never interviewed a psychologist.*

Dr. Hartley: *Don't worry about it; we're ordinary men you know, one leg at a time.*

Ruth Corley: *Well, if I start to ramble a little or if I get into an area I'm not too conversant with, you'll help me out, won't you?*

Dr. Hartley: *Don't worry about it. If you get into trouble, just turn it over to me and I'll wing it.*

Augie (Voice Over): *10 seconds, Ruth!*

Ruth Corley: *Thanks, Augie.*

Dr. Hartley: *You'll be fine.*

Ruth Corley: *Here goes.*

Augie (VO): *3, 2, you're on.*

Ruth Corley: *Good morning. It's 7 o'clock, and I am Ruth Corley. My first guest is psychologist, Dr. Robert Hartley. It's been said that today's psychologist is nothing* *more than a con man; a snake oil salesman, flim-flamming innocent people, peddling cures for everything from nail bites to a lousy love life, and I agree. We will ask Dr. Hartley to defend himself after this message.*

Dr. Hartley: *Was that on the air?*

Ruth Corley: *Oh, that's just what we call a grabber. You know, it keeps the audience from tuning out.*

Augie (VO): *Ten seconds, Ruth.*

Ruth Corley: *Thanks, Augie.*

Dr. Hartley: *We won't be doing anymore grabbing will we?*

Ruth Corley: *No, no. From now on we'll just talk.*

Augie (VO): *3, 2, you're on.*

Ruth Corley: *Dr. Hartley, according to a recently published survey, the average fee for a private session with a psychologist is 40 dollars.*

Dr. Hartley: *That's about right.*

Ruth Corley: *Right? I don't think it's right! What other practitioner gets 40 dollars an hour?*

Dr. Hartley: *My plumber.*

Ruth Corley: *Plumbers guarantee their work, do you?*

Dr. Hartley: *See, I don't understand why all of the sudden…*

Ruth Corley: *I asked you if you guaranteed your work!*

Dr. Hartley: *Well, I can't guarantee each and every person that walks through the door is going to be cured.*

Ruth Corley: *You mean you ask 40 dollars an hour and you guarantee nothing?*

Dr. Hartley: *I validate.*

Ruth Corley: *Is that your answer?*

Dr Hartley: *Could…can I have a word with you?*

Ruth Corley: *Chicago is waiting for your answer!*

Dr. Hartley: *Well, Chicago…everyone that comes in doesn't pay 40 dollars an hour.*

Ruth Corley: *Do you ever cure anybody?*

Dr. Hartley: *Well, I wouldn't say cure.*

Ruth Corley: *So your answer is "No."*

Dr. Hartley: *No, no my answer is not "No." I get results. Many of my patients solve their problems and go on to become successful.*

Ruth Corley: *Successful at what?*

Dr. Hartley: *Professional athletes, clergyman, some go on to head large corporations. One of my patients is an elected official.*

Ruth Corley: *A WHAT?*

Dr. Hartley: *Nothing, nothing.*

Ruth Corley: *Did you say an elected official?*

Dr Hartley: *I might have, I forget.*

Ruth Corley: *Who is it?*

Dr. Hartley: *Well, I can't divulge his identity.*

Ruth Corley: *Why? There is a deranged man out there in a position of power!*

Dr. Hartley: *He isn't deranged…. Anymore.*

Ruth Corley: *But he was when he came to see you, and you said yourself that you do not give guarantees.*

Dr. Hartley: *Uh…*

Ruth Corley: *After this message we will meet our choice for woman of the year, Sister Mary Catherine.*

Augie (VO): *Okay, we're into commercial.*

Dr. Hartley: *Thanks, Augie.*

Ruth Corley: *Thank you, Dr Hartley. You were terrific. I mean, I wish we had more time.*

Dr. Hartley: *We had plenty.*

Ruth Corley: *Well, I really enjoyed it.*

Dr. Hartley: *You would have enjoyed Pearl Harbor.*

Ruth Corley: *Good morning, Sister. It's wonderful of you to come at this hour.*

Dr. Hartley: *If I were you I wouldn't get into religion, she will chew your legs off. [1.1]*

Newhart accompanied his uncertain verbal responses to the interviewer's attacks with an array of equally edgy physical behavior: He squirmed in his seat, he stammered, he twitched, his eyes darted up and down and around and around frantically, and he crossed his arms and legs protectively. But even without these visual images, his words alone depict a man desperately trying to cover his tracks. Despite all the humor, Bob Newhart came across as *defensive*.

Defensive, Evasive, or Contentious

Different people react differently to challenging questions. While some become defensive, others become *evasive*. A vivid example of the latter came at the end of a string of events that were set into motion on the evening of December 5, 2002.

Strom Thurmond, the Republican senator from South Carolina, with a long history of segregationist votes and opinions, reached his one-hundredth birthday. At a celebratory banquet on Capitol Hill in Washington D.C. on that fateful Thursday, Trent Lott, the Republican senator from Mississippi and then Senate Majority Leader, stood to honor his colleague. During his remarks, Senator Lott said:

> *When Strom Thurmond ran for President, we voted for him. We're proud of it. And if the rest of the country had followed our lead, we wouldn't have had all these problems over all these years, either.*

The statement created an uproar that raged like wildfire across the country. Five days later, even the pro-Republican *The Wall Street Journal* ran an editorial condemning the statement. In an attempt to quell the furor, Lott issued a two-sentence written apology on December 10.

> *A poor choice of words conveyed to some the impression that I embraced the discarded policies of the past. Nothing could be further from the truth, and I apologize to anyone who was offended by my statement.*

The statement failed to stem the continuing public outcry. A week later, in what he thought would be a bold step to make amends, Lott agreed to appear on Black Entertainment Television. He was interviewed by anchor Ed Gordon, who went right to the heart of the matter. At the very start of the program, Gordon pushed the hot button by asking the senator to explain what he meant by "all of those problems" in his original statement.

Lott responded with a wide array of problems, none of which addressed Gordon's question.

Gordon interrupted Lott's rambling, evasive answer to remind him that Thurmond was also a strong proponent of segregation.

Lott tried to change the subject but Gordon pressed him as to whether he knew that Thurmond was a segregationist. Lott finally capitulated. True to his journalistic profession, Gordon immediately followed with another question seeking confirmation that Lott understood.

Unable to evade any longer, Lott capitulated again.

Politicians are not the only people who become evasive under fire; such behavior extends even to sports. Pedro Martinez, one of the most dominant pitchers in Major League Baseball, provides a case in point. After seven successful years with the Boston Red Sox, culminating in a dramatic World Series victory in 2004, Martinez decided to leave his team to join the New York Mets, a dismal team with a losing record. In an effort to reverse their fortunes, the Mets outbid the Red Sox with a four-year contract for the pitcher worth $54 million.

When he arrived in New York, Martinez held a press conference filled with cynical sports reporters who bombarded him with tough questions about his decision, one of which was

> *What about people who think this is all about you taking the money? That is the general perception in Boston now.*

Martinez answered,

> *They are totally wrong, because I was a millionaire, I had already achieved a lot of money. I'm a wealthy man since I got to Boston. Like I said before, in the press conference today, when I got to Boston, I was making millions. Every million, every minute in the big leagues, is more than I had ever in my life. I'm a millionaire once I got to the big leagues. Money's not my issue, but respect is, and that's what Boston lacked to show by not showing interest. They're going to make it look like it was the money. Now my question would be, "Why did they have to wait until the last moment to make a move, until I had committed to another place?"[1.2]*

To answer a question about money with an answer about timing and respect is not much better than answering a question about segregation with an answer about fighting Nazism and Communism. It is equally evasive.

After evasiveness and defensiveness, the third variation on the theme of negative responses to challenging questions is *contentiousness*. One of the most combative men ever to enter the political arena is H. Ross Perot, the billionaire businessman, who has a reputation for cantankerousness. In 1992, Perot ran for president as an independent candidate and, although he conducted an aggressive campaign, lost to Bill Clinton. The following year, Perot continued to act the gadfly by leading the opposition to the Clinton-backed North American Free Trade Agreement (NAFTA). Matters came to a head on the night of November 9, 1993, when Perot engaged then Vice President Al Gore in a rancorous debate on Larry King's television program.

In the heat of battle, Perot launched into the subject of lobbying.

> *You know what the problem is, folks? It's foreign lobbyists... are wreckin' this whole thing. Right here,* Time Magazine *just says it all, it says "In spite of Clinton's protests, the influence-peddling machine in Washington is back in high gear." The headline,* Time Magazine*: "A Lobbyist's Paradise."*

Gore tried to interject.

> *I'd like to respond to that.*

Larry King tried to allow Gore to speak.

> *All right, let him respond.*

Perot barreled ahead, his forefinger wagging at the camera...and the audience.

> *We are being sold out by foreign lobbyists. We've got 33 of them working on this in the biggest lobbying effort in the history of our country to ram NAFTA down your throat.*

Gore tried to interject again.

> *I'd like to respond...*

But Perot had one more salvo.

That's the bad news. The good news is it ain't working.

Having made his point, Perot leaned forward to the camera, smiled smugly, and turned the floor back to Gore.

I'll turn it over to the others.

Larry King made the hand-off.

OK, Ross.

Gore took his turn.

OK, thank you. One of President Clinton's first acts in office was to put limits on the lobbyists and new ethics laws, and we're working for lobby law reform right now. But, you know, we had a little conversation about this earlier, but every dollar that's been spent for NAFTA has been publicly disclosed. We don't know yet... tomorrow...perhaps tomorrow we'll see, but the reason why...and I say this respectfully because I served in the Congress and I don't know of any single individual who lobbied the Congress more than you did, or people in your behalf did, to get tax breaks for your companies. And it's legal.

Perot bristled and shot back.

You're lying! You're lying now!

"You're lying!" is as contentious as a statement can be. True to form, Perot showed his belligerence. Gore looked incredulously at Perot.

You didn't lobby the Ways and Means Committee for tax breaks for yourself and your companies?

Perot stiffened.

> *What do you have in mind? What are you talking about?*

Gore said matter-of-factly,

> *Well, it's been written about extensively and again, there's nothing illegal about it.*

Perot sputtered, disdainfully.

> *Well that's not the point! I mean, what are you talking about?*

With utter calm, Gore replied,

> *Lobbying the Congress. You know a lot about it.*

Now Perot was livid. He glowered at Gore and insisted,

> *I mean, spell it out, spell it out!*

Gore pressed his case.

> *You didn't lobby the Ways and Means Committee? You didn't have people lobbying the Ways and Means Committee for tax breaks?*

Contemptuous, Perot stood his ground.

> *What are you talking about?*

Gore tried to clarify.

> *In the 1970s…*

Perot pressed back.

> *Well, keep going.*

Now Gore sat up, looked Perot straight in the eye, and asked his most direct challenging question.

Well, did you or did you did you not? I mean, it's not...

His back against the wall, Perot fought back.

Well, you're so general I can't pin it down! [1.3]

The adjectives *defensive, evasive,* and *contentious* are synonymous with "Fight or Flight," the human body's instinctive reaction to stress. In each of the cases above, Fight or Flight was the response to tough questions: Ross Perot became as pugnacious as a bare-knuckled street fighter; Trent Lott danced around as if he were standing on a bed of burning coals; and Bob Newhart's jumping jack antics looked like a man desperately trying to eject from his hot seat.

Presenter Behavior/ Audience Perception

While Bob Newhart's words and behavior produced a comic effect, any such response in business or social situations would produce dire consequences. A presenter or speaker who exhibits negative behavior produces a negative impression on the audience. This correlation is a critical factor with far-reaching implications in *any* communication setting, particularly so in the mass media.

Pedro Martinez's behavior produced reams of caustic cynical reaction in the press, and even stronger criticism on the Internet. The day after his press conference, the fan chat boards lit up with vituperative messages, several of which referred to the pitcher as "Paydro."

While Martinez went on to join the Mets unaffected, Trent Lott did not get off so lightly. His behavior on Black Entertainment Television had a profound effect on public opinion. The week after his appearance, with the furor unabated, a disgraced Lott resigned his position as Senate Majority Leader.

Ross Perot's behavior on the Larry King program also had a profound effect on public opinion. Figure 1.1 shows the results of polls taken on the day before and the day after the debate.

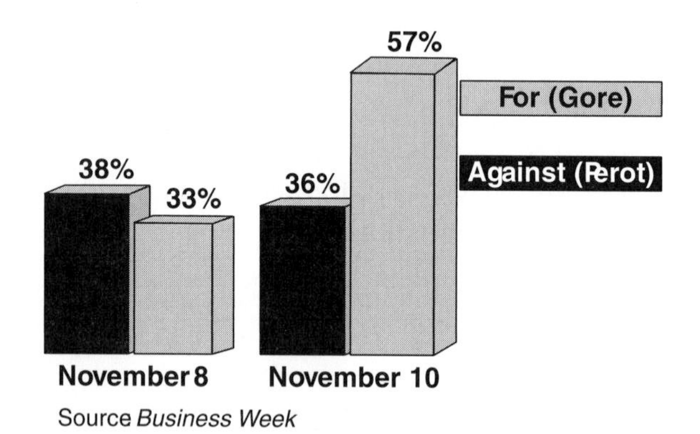

FIGURE 1.1 *1993 NAFTA public opinion polls. (Reprinted by permission of* Business Week.*)*

In the 48 hours between the two polls, the only factor with any impact on the NAFTA issue was the debate on the Larry King program. It had to be Ross Perot's contentious behavior that swung the undecided respondents against his cause.

One final example of negative behavior in response to challenging questions comes from that most challenging of all business communications, an IPO road show. When companies go public, the chief officers develop a presentation that they take on the road to deliver to investors in about a dozen cities, over a period of two weeks, making their pitch up to 10 times day for a total of 60 to 80 iterations.

The company in this particular case had a very successful business. They had accumulated 16 consecutive quarters of profitability. Theirs was a very simple business concept: a software product that they sold directly into the retail market. The CEO, having made many presentations over the years to his consumer constituency, as well as to his industry peers, was a very proficient presenter. At the start of the road show, the anticipated price range of the company's offering was nine to eleven dollars per share.

However, the CEO, having presented primarily to receptive audiences, was unaccustomed to the kind of tough questions investors ask. Every time his potential investors challenged him, he responded with halting and uncertain answers.

After the road show, the opening price of the company's stock was nine dollars a share, the bottom of the offering range. Given the three million shares offered, the swing cost the company six million dollars.

The conclusion from the foregoing harkens back to David Bellet's observation that investors are not seeking an education; they are looking to see how a presenter stands up in the line of fire. Investors kick the tires to see how the management responds to adversity. Audiences kick tires to assess a presenter's mettle. Employers kick the tires of prospective employees to test their grit. In all these challenging exchanges, the presenter must exhibit positive behavior that creates a positive impression on the audience.

The first steps in learning how to behave effectively begin in the next chapter.

CHAPTER 2

Effective Management *Implemented*

Worst Case Scenario

Soldiers prepare for battle by conducting realistic maneuvers. Athletes prepare for competition by practicing with extra resistance or weights. Politicians prepare for debates by staging mock rehearsals with skilled stand-ins for their opponents.

In preparing you to step into the line of fire when you open the floor to questions, let's assume the worst case scenario: that all the questions you will be asked will be the *most* hostile possible...like those Ruth Corley flung at Bob Newhart or like those Mike Wallace fired at thousands of interviewees. If you can learn to handle that caliber of ammunition, you can learn to handle any question.

To raise the bar even further, let's assume that all your Q&A sessions will be conducted in large groups: the one-against-many dynamic. If you can survive those odds, you will be able to handle any question in any encounter...even one-to-one.

Maximum Control in Groups

In most large group settings with 50 or more people in the audience, the presenter usually has a microphone, and the audience does not, which allows the presenter to deliver the full presentation uninterrupted. In this situation, the audience members usually hold their questions to the end. In small group settings, the opposite is true; because of the informality and immediacy, the audience members freely ask questions at any time during the presentation, which usually turns the presentation into discussion. Nevertheless, in each setting, the presenter must *always* remain in control whenever a question is asked.

Let's start with the large group. At the end of a presentation, the presenter opens the floor to questions and then proceeds to step through the following inflection points:

- Open the floor
- Recognize the questioner
- Yield the floor
- Retake the floor
- Provide an answer

After the answer, the cycle starts again and continues on to another member of the audience, and then another, in recurrent clockwise cycles.

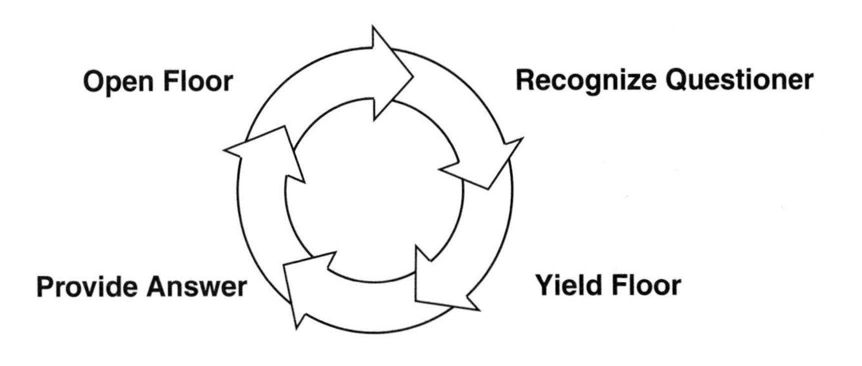

▲ **FIGURE 2.1** *The Q&A cycle.*

The Q&A Cycle

Each of the steps in the cycle provides an opportunity to exercise control, and as you will see, those control measures are applicable to both large and small groups.

Open the Floor

Control the Time

When the presentation is done and you open the floor to questions, say, "We have time for only a few questions," "I've got to catch a plane and don't have time for questions," "We'll take all your questions in the breakout session," or "I'll be here for the rest of the afternoon to answer any question you might have." It doesn't matter what you say. It matters that you say it up front and set expectations.

Exert time management.

Then, as you get closer to the end of your Q&A session, fulfill your forecast by starting to count down: "Three more questions," "Two more," "One more," "Last question." Exert time management.

Control the Traffic

In what is very likely a carryover from grade school, most people in large groups almost always raise their hands when they want to speak. That practice often carries forward in small groups. You can leverage that custom by raising your hand when you start your Q&A session, implicitly inviting your audience members to raise theirs if they want to be recognized. When you open the floor, raise your hand and say, "Who has a question?" Your audience might not comply and launch right into a question, but you have a better chance if you establish this signal. Of course, this tactic is only appropriate in audiences where there is a peer relationship. Do *not* raise your hand when standing in front of a group of potential investors or the Board of Directors.

In small groups, all bets are off. The informality of these sessions makes these suggestions null and void. In these cases, skip the first step and advance to the second.

Recognize the Questioner

Let's say three hands go up at some point either during or after your presentation. You get to choose which one to recognize. *Use an open hand and do not point.* All too often, presenters or speakers point to indicate their selection. This is perfectly acceptable in a bakery, but not in presentations. To avoid this unconscious tendency in your Q&A sessions, exercise a simple arithmetic equation: one plus three. Extend your forefinger, but roll out the other three fingers to create an open palm. Receive your questioners openly.

Use an open hand and do not point.

In presidential press conferences, tradition has it that the president addresses a few select reporters by name. You are not the president of the United States. You might be the president of your company, but you do not have the same privileges.

For instance, let's say you know John, but you don't know the man seated behind him. You recognize John first and call him by name. Then you recognize the man behind John and call him "Sir." The second man will feel the outsider.

Take the same circumstances but reverse the order. The first person you recognize is the man behind John, and you call him "Sir." No problem. Then you recognize John, and call him "Sir," too. Because you know John, you are not offending him.

The ground rule is: *If you know the name of every person in the room, call everyone by name. If you do not know the name of every person in the room, call no one by name.* If you call the names of only selected people, you run the risk of implying favoritism at least and collusion at worst.

Yield the Floor

Let's say that you recognize the gentleman or the woman in the middle of the back of the room, and you now yield the floor to that person. This is a very big moment. Your motor has been running at full speed delivering your presentation. During that entire time, that audience member's motor has been idle. You step on the brakes and screech to a halt, and that person's motor suddenly lurches into motion.

How do most people ask questions...clear, crisp and succinct? No, most of the time their questions are long and rambling. Why?

Is it because your audiences are not very bright? No, it is because they have just taken in a great deal of information and are still processing *your* ideas, most of which are new to them. Furthermore, all this mental activity occurs primarily in the right hemisphere of the brain, which happens to process data in a non-linear sequence. Finally, by suddenly becoming the focus of attention for the rest of the audience, the questioner becomes nervous and exhibits the harried symptoms of Fight or Flight. That person's ill-formed thoughts then come tumbling out in a disjointed, run-on statement, which may or may not even take the form of a question.

In the meantime, you, who are very knowledgeable and very clear about your own subject matter, receive your questioner's discursive statement in heightened state of alertness and perceive it as confused. All these diametrically opposite dynamics can produce dramatic results.

How to Lose Your Audience in Five Seconds Flat

Try this exercise: Stand up and ask a seated colleague to ask you a long, rambling question on any subject. It can be about the weather, the news, or your business. Ask that person to keep their eyes fixed on you as they ramble. Shortly after they start, thrust your hands into your pockets and settle back onto one foot. Watch what happens. Usually, the person's ramble will start to sputter and slow down. Ask the person how your slouch felt to them, and they will very likely say that it felt as if you weren't listening.

I do this exercise in my private sessions with my clients, and they tell me, "You look like you weren't interested," "You were bored," "You were being impatient," or "You could care less."

When a presenter sends that kind of message to an audience, the effect can be devastating. That moment arrests all forward progress. All communication stops. You cannot even contemplate proceeding to the next two vital inflection points in the Q&A cycle (Figure 2.1): Retake the floor and Provide the answer. In fact, we will defer any consideration of these points for two entire chapters until you learn what to do when you yield the floor: Listen effectively.

CHAPTER

3

You're *Not* Listening!

Falstaff: "It is the disease of not listening, the malady of not marking, that I am troubled withal."

2 Henry IV, Act I, Scene ii
by William Shakespeare

Breathes there a man or woman who has not accused or been accused by their significant other of not listening? Highly doubtful. The opprobrium of not listening ranks high among the causes of failure in human communication; it spans interpersonal, business, political, and even international relations. To the perpetrators of what troubled Falstaff, listening is merely a matter of waiting to speak.

For the *reductio ad absurdum* of this universal truth, think of a time when you were in a restaurant where you have given your waiter explicit instructions to exclude garlic, bacon, or butter from your meal, only to have your meal arrive reeking of garlic, littered with bacon bits, or swimming in butter. The waiter will suffer, at best, a return trip to the kitchen or, at worst, a diminished tip.

Notch the stakes up to interpersonal communications, and the consequence can be an argument at best or a severe strain on the relationship at worst. In business, the consequence can be failure to close the deal, gain approval, or get the investment. Remember the example in Chapter 1, "The Critical Dynamics of Q&A," of the lower share price of the Initial Public Offering due to the CEO's poor handling of questions.

Why would anyone in a mission-critical communication setting risk such a fate? The paradoxical reason is that most people in business, being results-driven by nature *and* nurture *and* culture, respond promptly to questions with answers. With good intentions, and seemingly efficient behavior, they rush to bring an open question to resolution. To further their cause, they often retain professional communication consultants, public relations advisors, or media coaches to help them prepare to open the floor to audience queries by compiling a long list of tough questions and a parallel list of canned answers in what is known as "Rude Q&A."

A more apt name is "Wrong Q&A," for if your answer is formulated before the key issue in the question *as asked* is crystal clear to you, your prepared answer might not match. This very likely will propel you into a desperate mental scramble to find a match and result in a wrong answer. Your wrong answer will then result in an audience reaction that virtually shouts, "You're *not* listening!"

A dramatic case in point of this vicious cycle occurred on October 15, 1992, in the second presidential debate among George H. Bush, the incumbent president, and his challengers, Bill Clinton, the then-governor of Arkansas, and H. Ross Perot, the billionaire businessman with a reputation for arrogance and belligerence. The leading contenders were each struggling with challenging issues: President Bush with a down economy and Governor Clinton with recent revelations of an extramarital affair, marijuana use, and anti-Vietnam war protests.

All three candidates gathered in the Robbins Field House at University of Richmond in Virginia to engage in the first-ever town hall format in which they were to answer questions posed by ordinary citizens. Carole Simpson, an ABC Television journalist, was the moderator, and one of the citizens she recognized was a twenty-six year-old black woman named Marisa Hall.

A technician brought a hand microphone to Marisa Hall, who asked:

> *Yes. How has the national debt personally affected each of your lives?*

As she was asking her question, President Bush looked at his wristwatch, as seen in Figure 3.1.

▲ **FIGURE 3.1** *George H. Bush looking at his watch during a presidential debate.*

Marisa Hall continued:

> *...And if it hasn't, how can you honestly find a cure for the economic problems of the common people if you have no experience in what's ailing them?*

President Bush began his answer:

> *Well, I think the national debt affects everybody. Obviously...*

Her microphone still open, Marisa Hall said:

> *You personally.*

She said "You personally." George H. Bush, said "everybody." He wasn't listening. Stopped in his tracks, he tried to recover.

> *...it has a lot to do with interest rates. It has...*

The moderator interjected:

She's saying, "you personally."

Marisa Hall tried to clarify her question.

You, on a personal basis...how has it affected you?

Carole Simpson tried to help.

Has it affected you personally?

President Bush replied:

I'm sure it has. I love my grandchildren. I want to think that...

Marisa Hall's soft voice, amplified by the live microphone, rose above the exchange to resound through the Robbins Field House public address system, out along a vast network of coaxial cables to television transmitters, across the United States into millions of television receivers and into banks of video tape recorders that captured her word for posterity.

How?

This was the second time that she asked the question and President Bush still didn't understand. He tried to answer again.

I want to think that they're going to be able to afford an education. I think that that's an important part of being a parent. If the question...maybe I...get it wrong. Are you suggesting that if somebody has means that the national debt doesn't affect them?

Three times and he still didn't have it. The young woman tried to clarify again, her voice rising ever so slightly.

Well, what I'm saying is...

President Bush finally gave up.

I'm not sure I get...help me with the question and I'll try to answer it.

It took four attempts until he admitted that he didn't understand her question. The young woman tried to help by elaborating.

Well, I've had friends that have been laid off from jobs.

Despite a fretful expression on his face, the President tried to sound attentive.

Yeah.

The young woman continued.

I know people who cannot afford to pay the mortgage on their homes...their car payment. I have personal problems with the national debt. But how has it affected you and if you have no experience in it, how can you help us, if you don't know what we're feeling?

President Bush still seemed puzzled, so Carole Simpson intervened again.

I think she means more the recession...the economic problems today the country faces rather than the deficit.

Now clearer, President Bush launched into his answer.

Well, listen, you ought to be in the White House for a day and hear what I hear and see what I see and read the mail I read and touch the people that I touch from time to time. I was in the Lomax AME Church. It's a black church just outside of Washington, DC. And I read in the bulletin about teenage pregnancies, about the difficulties that families are having to make ends meet. I talk to parents. I mean, you've got to care. Everybody cares if people aren't doing well.

His voice rising defensively, he continued.

> *But I don't think it's fair to say, you haven't had cancer. Therefore, you don't know what it's like. I don't think it's fair to say, you know, whatever it is, that if you haven't been hit by it personally. But everybody's affected by the debt because of the tremendous interest that goes into paying on that debt everything's more expensive. Everything comes out of your pocket and my pocket. So it's that.*
>
> *But I think in terms of the recession, of course you feel it when you're president of the US. And that's why I'm trying to do something about it by stimulating the export, vesting more, better education systems.*
>
> *Thank you. I'm glad to clarify it. [3.1]*

But he didn't clarify it. President Bush's long, circuitous route to answer the young woman's question created the distinct impression that he either wasn't listening or was completely out of touch. This negative impression compounded and exacerbated a similar impression he had made just eight months before this painful exchange. In February of 1992, the president paid a visit to the National Grocers Association convention in Orlando, Florida, where he was shown a common electronic bar code scanner. According to reports in several newspapers, he seemed amazed to learn about a product that had been in supermarkets since the 1980s.

James Carville, Clinton's campaign manager, seized upon the bar code scanner episode and magnified it to major proportions with his notorious slogan, "It's the economy, stupid." To a nation mired in an economic downturn, Marisa Hall's question was right on target. It was also to become the point of no return for George H. Bush, as the public opinion polls show in Figure 3.2.

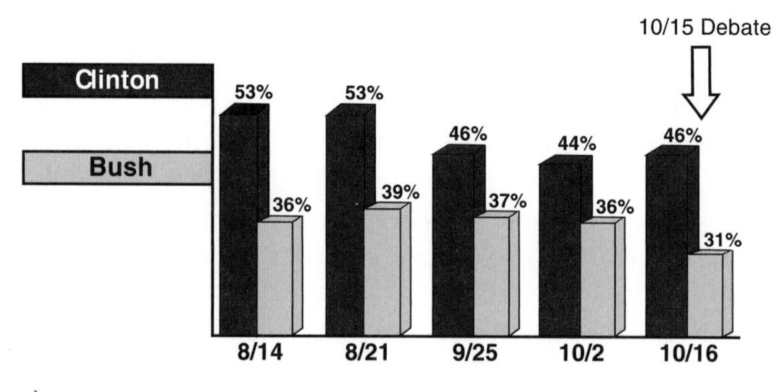

▲ **FIGURE 3.2** *1992 Presidential public opinion polls. [3.2]*

Politicians consider the day after the last major party nominating convention to be the formal start of presidential election campaigns. In 1992, when the Republican Convention ended (8/14), Clinton had surged into a 17-point lead over Bush for a variety of reasons, high among them the troubled economy. Moreover, given that the Democratic Convention preceded the Republican Convention that year, the media exposure benefited the challenger. This is known in the political trade as "bounce."

As so often happens, in the week following the Republican Convention (8/21), Bush, with his own media exposure, got his own "bounce" and began to close the gap between himself and Clinton to 14 points. Over the next several weeks, (9/25 through 10/2), Bush held steady in the polls. During that same period, Ross Perot became a candidate, causing Clinton's numbers to drop precipitously to only an 8-point lead over Bush. By the beginning of October, the campaign had turned into a horse race. Then on October 15, the town hall debate took place, and Marisa Hall asked her fateful question. The very next day, the numbers for Bush and Clinton began to diverge and continued in those directions until Election Day in November.

James Carville, reflecting on the impact of Miss Hall's question in his memoir of the campaign said, "I would have *paid* to have that question asked!" [3.3]

Never again would such an incident occur in presidential debates. Four years later in 1996, the candidates eliminated follow-on questions *de facto*. President Bill Clinton and Senator Bob Dole, two highly skilled debaters, were such good listeners that, in their town-hall format, none of the citizens asked a single follow-on question. Both candidates always got the key issue and threaded the needle with their answers from their respective points of view.

Four years later, in 2000, the possibility of follow-on questions was eliminated *de jure*. When George H. Bush's son, George W. Bush, participated in the same open town-hall format (against then-Vice President Al Gore), the rules changed. At the start of that year's debate, the moderator, the veteran PBS newsman, Jim Lehrer, announced:

> *The audience participants are bound by the following rule: they shall not ask follow-up questions or otherwise participate in the extended discussion and the questioner's microphone will be turned off after he or she completes asking the question. Those are the rules. [3.4]*

Four years later, in 2004, when President George W. Bush committed to another town-hall debate format (this time against Senator John F. Kerry), his representatives set even more rigorous ground rules in advance. The moderator, Charles Gibson of ABC News, announced them at the start of the debate on October 8, 2004.

> *Earlier today, each audience member gave me two questions on cards like this, one they'd like to ask the president, the other they'd like to ask the senator. I have selected the questions to be asked and the order. No one has seen the final list of questions but me, certainly not the candidates. No audience member knows if he or she will be called upon. Audience microphones will be turned off after a question is asked. [3.5]*

In 1992, of course, Marisa Hall's microphone was left open for all the world to hear her resounding "How?" As decisive and as devastating as the events resulting from her follow-on question appear, they were even worse for George H. Bush. Yes, he did look at his wristwatch as she asked her question and sent the message that he wasn't listening, but *after* he looked at his watch he had another 55 seconds to formulate a better response. That interval was occupied by Ross Perot's answer. Miss Hall's question was addressed to all three men, and Perot went first.

As soon as the young woman finished asking her question, Perot volunteered:

> *May I answer that?*

The moderator approved.

> *Well, Mr. Perot...yes, of course.*

Perot asked:

> *Who do you want to start with?*

Marisa Hall explained:

> *My question is for each of you, so...*

Perot took the floor.

> *It caused me to disrupt my private life and my business to get involved in this activity. That's how much I care about it. And believe me, if you knew my family and if you knew the private life I have, you would agree in a minute that that's a whole lot more fun than getting involved in politics.*
>
> *But I have lived the American dream. I came from very modest background. Nobody's been luckier than I've been, all the way across the spectrum, and the greatest riches of all are my wife and children. That's true of any*

family. But I want all the children...I want these young people up here to be able to start with nothing but an idea like I did and build a business. But they've got to have a strong basic economy and if you're in debt, it's like having a ball and chain around you. I just figure, as lucky as I've been, I owe it to them and I owe it to the future generations and on a very personal basis, I owe it to my children and grandchildren. [3.6]

Despite Perot's succinct, empathic, and relevant answer, George H. Bush took his turn next with an answer that was far enough off target to invite interruption...three interruptions...and create the distinct perception that he *wasn't listening*.

It got still worse for President Bush. Following his rambling answer and awkward exchange with Miss Hall, Bill Clinton's turn came. As Bush headed back to his stool, the challenger rose from his and walked toward Miss Hill, addressing her directly:

Tell me how it's affected you again.

His approach put Miss Hall at a momentary loss for words.

Um...

Continuing toward her, Clinton prodded her memory.

You know people who've lost their jobs and lost their homes?

Marisa Hall agreed.

Well, yeah, uh-huh.

"Well, yeah, uh-huh." She could just as well have said, "You *were* listening!" In that one pivotal moment, Bill Clinton became the complete opposite of George H. Bush. In that one pivotal moment, the die was cast for the dark horse challenger's victory at the expense of the incumbent.

The moment was a long time in the making. Clinton's movement, eye contact, and body language were fully intentional. As James Carville described in his memoir, "We did practice having the governor get off his stool and walk down to make contact with the man or woman asking the question...we would always remind him, 'Go talk to that person. Be engaged in what he has to say.'" [3.7]

There was also the matter of Clinton's words. One month after President Bush's moment with the bar code scanner that worked against him, Clinton faced a challenging moment of his own that he turned into an advantage. On March 26, 1992, Clinton appeared at a political fund raiser in New York. During his speech, Bob Rafsky, a member of an organization called AIDS Coalition to Unleash Power, or ACT UP, interrupted and accused Clinton of not doing enough to combat AIDS. Clinton departed from his speech to respond to Rafsky, and the exchange became heated. For a short while, the two went toe-to-toe, but Clinton finally put an end to the quarrel when he said, "I've got friends who have died of AIDS. *I feel your pain.*" [3.8]

"I feel your pain." Early on in his run for office, Bill Clinton saw and understood the power of those four words. They were to become the leitmotif of his campaign and the engine he would ride to victory and the White House. The underlying implication in those words is not only "I heard you," but also, and more importantly, "I care about you."

As soon as Bill Clinton heard Marisa Hall say, "Well, yeah, uh-huh," he picked up the ball and ran with it.

> *Well, I've been governor of a small state for 12 years. I'll tell you how it's affected me. Every year Congress and the president sign laws that make us do more things and gives us less money to do it with.*

Now Clinton shifted into overdrive. He made his entire point of view identical with that of Marisa Hall's.

I see people in my state, middle class people...their taxes have gone up in Washington and their services have gone down while the wealthy have gotten tax cuts. I have seen what's happened in this last four years when...in my state, when people lose their jobs there's a good chance I'll know them by their names. When a factory closes, I know the people who ran it. When the businesses go bankrupt, I know them.

And I've been out here for 13 months meeting in meetings just like this ever since October, with people like you all over America...

When Clinton said, "people like you," Marisa Hall nodded her head silently. She could just as well have lifted her microphone again and said, "You *were* listening!"

Just then, the live television broadcast cut to a close two-shot of Clinton and Marisa Hall, and captured her assenting nod (see Figure 3.3).

▲ **FIGURE 3.3** *Bill Clinton answers Marisa Hall's question.*

Bill Clinton rolled on.

> *...people that have lost their jobs, lost their livelihood, lost their health insurance. What I want you to understand is the national debt is not the only cause of that.*

Even though Carole Simpson had, during President Bush's answer, tactfully and tacitly corrected Miss Hall's confusion of the national debt with the recession, Clinton took the opportunity to repeat the young woman's original words...*the national debt*...and, in so doing, further validated her. Then he answered her.

> *It is because America has not invested in its people. It is because we have not grown. It is because we've had 12 years of trickle down economics. We've gone from first to twelfth in the world in wages. We've had four years where we've produced no private sector jobs. Most people are working harder for less money than they were making ten years ago.*
>
> *It is because we are in the grip of a failed economic theory. And this decision you're about to make better be about what kind of economic theory you want, not just people saying I'm going to go fix it but what are we going to do? I think what we have to do is invest in American jobs, American education, control American health care costs and bring the American people together again. [3.9]*

The chain reaction of repercussions that nullified George H. Bush's bid for re-election can be traced back to a single pivotal moment: providing the wrong answer to a question. That moment was marked "at Virginia Commonwealth University [where] 105 uncommitted voters watched the proceedings with 'debate meters' in hand, instantly recording when they had a positive or negative reaction to what the candidates were saying. Bush scored one of his two most negative responses of the evening with his answer to Hall." [3.10]

That moment also was marked by Marisa Hall. After the debate she said, "President Bush never answered it. It kind of upset me. He started talking about going to that black church, and then he started talking about his grandchildren." She voted for Clinton. [3.11]

George H. Bush's fumbled answer, which set in motion an avalanche that brought down the house of the 41st Presidency, was a classic example of the critical blunder: "Ready, Fire, Aim!" He pulled the trigger before he had the target in his sights.

While very few people get the opportunity to try to win the Presidency of the United States, every one who tries to win in business and, in fact, everyone who tries to win in any endeavor by seeking the concurrence of other people, must avoid the fatal mistake of not listening. The remedy is a seemingly simple but deceptively counter-intuitive two-step solution:

- Listen correctly
- Answer properly

In the next chapter, you will learn the first step with a skill called *Active Listening*...and how close the first President Bush came to getting Marisa Hall's question right. In the succeeding chapters, you will learn how to answer properly and by Chapter Six, how George H. Bush might have answered her differently.

This delay in providing you with prescriptive instruction about answers is completely intentional. It is specifically designed to drive a deep wedge between the tough question and your answer. When you learn just what to do in that gap, you will be able to avoid the all-too-common malady that troubled Falstaff, will trouble your audience, and ultimately will trouble your cause.

CHAPTER 4

Active Listening

(Martial Art: Concentration)

Let me tell you a story…about the Japanese Zen Master who received a university professor who came to inquire about Zen. It was obvious to the master from the start of the conversation that the professor was not so much interested in learning about Zen as he was in impressing the master with his own opinions and knowledge. The master listened patiently and finally suggested that they have tea. The master poured his visitor's cup full and then kept pouring.

The professor watched the cup overflowing until he could no longer restrain himself. "The cup is overfull, no more will go in!"

"Like this cup," the master said, "you are full of your own opinions and speculations. How can I show you Zen unless you first empty your cup?"

Zen in the Martial Arts [4.1]

Let's flash forward to the end of your next mission-critical presentation and assume that it was the performance of a lifetime. Everything went perfectly: Your narrative was eloquent, your Microsoft PowerPoint slides were illustrative, your delivery was expressive, and your audience watched and listened in spellbound silence.

Now you open the floor to questions and you call on the gentleman in the middle of the back of the room. This is the moment of suspended animation we left at the end of Chapter 2, "Effective Management *Implemented*," which was **Yield the Floor**.

The man starts asking a question, but it sounds like Greek to you. You can tell that it has something to do with the material you just delivered, but the point of his rambling question is unclear. Being a results-driven person, you are eager to provide an answer.

That is precisely what happened to George H. Bush. He wanted to provide an answer to Marisa Hall, except that the answer he gave was not to the question she asked. She did not ask about his grandchildren or teenage pregnancies, nor did she ask about a black church just outside of Washington, D.C. What *did* she want to know? What should President Bush have done instead of answering?

Heed the advice of the Zen master: *Empty your cup*. Empty your mind of all your thoughts so that you can fill it instead with those of the questioner. *Concentrate.*

Concentration is essential in every activity in the human experience, particularly in athletic endeavors, and even more particularly in the martial arts where mortality is at stake. This was vividly illustrated in the 2003 film, "The Last Samurai," in which Tom Cruise played an American soldier, who in his quest to become a Samurai warrior, learns to fight with a lethal sword. Director Edward Zwick captured Cruise's intense concentration by first shooting the swordfight in wide angles until a pivotal moment and then by replaying the same scene from Cruise's close-up point of view. When Cruise observes the same pivotal moment, he watches his opponent's actions in extreme slow motion, sees a fault, and understands how to defeat him. His concentration brought him victory.

During your Q&A session, concentrate on your questioner's pivotal words as if in slow motion. This will be difficult to do in the heat of battle and under the glare of attention of the audience. It was difficult for Bill Clinton, the winner of the 1992 Presidential Debate *and* the election:

> *You know, it's not easy to listen to people anytime. It's a lot easier to be a good talker than a good listener. But in that format, with all that pressure, with one hundred million people watching, it's probably even harder to be a good listener. I saw the American people sort of screaming for me to pay attention to them and listen to them. [4.2]*

The solution: Step on the brakes. Avoid the "Ready, Fire, Aim!" trap. *Resist thinking of the answer and instead listen for the key issue. Concentrate.* Listen for the one or two words that identify the essence of the question, the heart of the matter.

Resist thinking of the answer and instead listen for the key issue.

Unfortunately, the key issue comes all wrapped up in a large knotty ball. One of the strands of that ball is misinformation. Marisa Hall had confused the national debt and the recession, and Carole Simpson, the moderator, tried to clarify by defining the terms.

> *I think she means more the recession...the economic problems today the country faces rather than the deficit.*

Despite Ms. Simpson's well-meaning effort, she took the discussion off on a tangent, away from the central issue.

One of the other strands wrapping and masking Miss Hall's question was her emotion.

> *Well, I've had friends that have been laid off from jobs. I know people who cannot afford to pay the mortgage on their homes, their car payment.*

Other strands that can obscure the key issues in *any* question include:

- Nonlinear right brain thinking
- Unprepared extemporaneity
- Anxiety about standing up exposed in front of an audience

As a result of all these factors, most questions come tumbling out helter-skelter, wrapping a dense thicket of strands around the key issue, producing a stream of jumbled words that is completely unclear to the presenter.

The challenge for you, as it was for President Bush, is to unwrap the ball. Peel away all the strands until you can see the Roman Column.

The Roman Column

In the glory days of the Roman Empire, around 100 BCE, the great Roman orators, such as Cicero, spoke in the imposing Forum for hours on end without a note in their hands. They couldn't because the invention of paper in China was still a couple of hundred years away. Instead, these orators used the stately marble columns of the Roman Forum as memory triggers. As the orators strode around majestically delivering their rhetoric, they stopped at various columns and discoursed eloquently on particular themes. Each column represented the focal point for a cluster of related ideas. Before you open the floor to questions about your mission-critical presentation, you must find your own Roman Columns, find your key issues. (For a fuller discussion of Roman Columns and the techniques to define them, please see my previous Prentice Hall book, *Presenting to Win: The Art of Telling Your Story.*)

What was the Roman Column in Marisa Hall's question?

Please note that the balance of this page is blank. This is for you to stop and think, or to look back at the transcript of the question in the previous chapter and decide what her key issue was.

The operative word in Marisa Hall's question was "how," the very word that had stopped George H. Bush in his tracks during the debate. She wanted to know *how* each of the candidates could solve the nation's economic problems considering they had no personal experience with them. She also had another *how*...how those economic problems affected them. But this second *how*, although posed first, was subordinate to her primary concern: whether these three candidates...two of whom were multimillionaires and one a career politician with two terms as a governor...could provide solutions to the country's economic problems when they clearly had none of their own. This constitutes a *double* Roman Column: the first being the *effect* of the economic problems on each man and the second, their *ability* to deliver solutions.

Marisa Hall asked her question twice, stating "affect" each time, and referring to solutions first as "a cure" and then as "help." Her first time was while President George H. Bush was looking at his watch.

> *How has the national debt personally affected each of your lives? And if it hasn't, how can you honestly find a cure for the economic problems of the common people if you have no experience in what's ailing them?*

The second time was when, after four failed attempts, the president asked her to help him by clarifying her question, and she responded,

> *But how has it affected you and if you have no experience in it, how can you help us, if you don't know what we're feeling?*

Did you get the Roman Columns? Don't worry if you didn't. I show the videotape of that exchange to my private clients and stop the tape to ask them the same question I asked you. Many people have seen that tape, but only about a quarter of them get it right. The rest get sidetracked by the discussion of the national debt and recession. They think that the Roman column is *only* about how the national debt or recession has affected the candidates personally. This is close, but no cigar. The cigar is: How can you, given your comfortable situation, help us?

George H. Bush actually touched on Marisa Hall's main concern *twice* during his exchange with her. First, as he struggled to understand her question:

> *Are you suggesting that if somebody has means that the national debt doesn't affect them?*

But he couched his question about her question so defensively and negatively that he backed himself into a corner and could not extricate himself. Instead, he simply gave up and asked the young woman to restate her question. After she did, he circled around the ability issue again during his rambling answer:

> *I don't think it's fair to say, you haven't had cancer. Therefore, you don't know what it's like. I don't think it's fair to say, you know, whatever it is, that if you haven't been hit by it personally.*

Once again, the negative cast of his words…three "don'ts" and two "haven'ts"…put him into reverse gear, unable to turn his answer positive.

As a matter of fact, none of the three candidates dealt specifically with the question of his *ability*. They all went directly to their solutions; an acceptable shift given that Marisa Hall was seeking "a cure for the economic problems of the common people."

Bill Clinton heard both of Marisa's concerns loud and clear. He addressed each Roman Column, beginning his answer with the first: the effect.

> *Well, I've been governor of a small state for 12 years. I'll tell you how it's affected me…*

And concluded his answer with the second: his solutions, articulated by the action verb "do"…in four ways.

> *I think what we have to do is invest in American jobs, American education, control American health care costs and bring the American people together again.*

Ross Perot also heard Marisa clearly. He began his answer with her first issue: the effect.

> *It caused me to disrupt my private life and my business to get involved in this activity. That's how much I care about it.*

And concluded his answer with the second: his solution.

> *I want these young people up here to be able to start with nothing but an idea like I did and build a business. But they've got to have a strong basic economy.*

Actually, President Bush also offered his solutions at the end of his answer.

> *But I think in terms of the recession, of course you feel it when you're president of the US. And that's why I'm trying to do something about it by stimulating the export, vesting more, better education systems.*

But his "do" words came at the tail end of his one minute and ten second answer, after his false start, after four bungled attempts, two interruptions, a tangential discussion, and a digressive ramble, by which time it was far too late. Clinton and Perot did not get to their solutions until the ends of their answers either, but each of them started his answer in the first person, thereby empathizing with Marisa's concern. George H. Bush began his answer by going universal.

> *Well, I think the national debt affects everybody.*

By generalizing, the president, in effect, distanced himself from the economic problems. Worse, in doing so, he ignored one of Marisa Hall's Roman Columns, which evoked her fateful follow-on question and, in turn, sent the message that he wasn't listening. Imagine if George H. Bush had *begun* his answer with his last words.

> *I'm trying to do something about it by stimulating the export, vesting more, better education systems.*

When Bill Clinton came bounding off his stool toward Marisa Hall to ask her, "Tell me how it's *affected* you again?" he evoked her "Well, yeah, uh-huh," response. And when, three sentences later, he began his answer with, "I'll tell you how it's *affected* me…" he sent the message that he had listened.

Emulate Bill Clinton in your Q&A sessions: Listen carefully to your audience and evoke your own equivalent of "Well, yeah, uh-huh."

Listen carefully to your audience and evoke your own equivalent of "Well, yeah, uh-huh."

Sub-vocalization

A very simple method to enable your Active Listening is *sub-vocalization*. Speak to yourself under your breath. Silently say the words that represent the Roman Column. "He's asking about *competition*," or "She's concerned about the *cost*," or "He wants to know about the *timing*."

As a matter of fact, President Bush used a hybrid form of sub-vocalization in his third attempt to answer Marisa Hall's question. Speaking aloud, he asked rhetorically,

> *Are you suggesting that if somebody has means that the national debt doesn't affect them?*

That was only the subordinate half of what she was suggesting, so he got no "Well, yeah, uh-huh," as Bill Clinton did. Instead of continuing on to clarify the key issue, President Bush gave up.

> *I'm not sure I get...help me with the question and I'll try to answer it.*

The lesson for you is to listen carefully for the Roman Column and sub-vocalize to help formulate it. Think of the key words, the one or two nouns or verbs central to the questioner's issue, hear them in your mind, but do *not* answer.

Visual Listening

Another vital part of Active Listening is the physical expression of your attentiveness. Remember the exercise in Chapter 2 where you saw the negative effect of merely relaxing into a slouch while listening silently? Avoid this trap by keeping all the elements of your outward appearance as focused on the person asking the question as your inner workings are focused on processing his or her words.

- *Balanced stance.* Distribute your weight evenly on both your feet.
- *Eye Connect.* Lock your eyes on the questioner as if you are a laser beam.
- *Head nods.* Show that you are in receive mode.
- *Voice assent.* Utter a few "Uh-huhs" or "Mm-hmms."
- *Steady fingers.* Don't let your fingers twiddle or fidget. If they do, a simple remedy is to squeeze the tips of your fingers in a short burst of pressure. This will drain the tension out of your hands.

Now let's go back to the moment where you've yielded the floor to the man in the middle of the back of the room. And let's say that you've listened carefully, you've sub-vocalized intently, you've "Mm-hmmed" several times, and you've nodded your head repeatedly, but you *still* don't understand.

...You *Still* Don't Understand

It was at this very moment that President George H. Bush made the fatal mistake of moving past the point of not understanding and, in so doing, became guilty of the Zen master's accusation, *"You are full of your own opinions and speculations."* The President speculated:

> *Are you suggesting that if somebody has means that the national debt doesn't affect them?*

Since he was off the mark, Marisa Hall started to correct him:

> *Well, what I'm saying is...[4.3]*

Her voice rose on the word "saying," indicating her frustration and therefore echoing...as well as validating...James Carville's "It's the economy, stupid" slogan. A close cousin of Ms. Hall's vocal exasperation is the more common, "Well, what I'm *really* asking..." in which the voice rises on the word "really." That irritable emphasis in the questioner's voice radiates out through the audience like wildfire. In the case of President Bush, the audience was the millions of people watching the debate and, ultimately, the majority of the electorate.

When some presenters don't understand the question, they make the mistake of trying to interpret. They say, "Let me see if I have this right..." which gives the questioner the opportunity to say, "No, you don't have it right!" The message is, *"You weren't listening!"*

Some presenters make the other mistake, known as the deafness ruse. They hear the question. Everyone else in the room hears the question, but the presenter, in an innocent tone of voice, says, "Could you repeat the question?" *The pretense is transparent.*

Other presenters go all the way to the end of their answer to a question that they didn't understand in the first place, and they see the narrowed eyes of the questioner glowering back at them. If the presenter, as far too many presenters do, then says, "Does that answer your question?" or its close cousin, "Is what you're asking...?" the questioner has the opportunity to say, "No." The message is, *"You weren't listening!"*

Remove these statements from your vocabulary.

- "Let me see if I have this right..."
- "Could you repeat the question?"
- "Does that answer your question?"
- "Is what you're asking...?"

If you do not *completely* understand the question...and completely means 100%, not 99.999%...picture a bold red line between you and your audience. Do *not* cross the line. Do *not* retake the floor. Do *not* answer. Do *not* interpret. Psychiatrists have difficulty interpreting veiled meanings. And as the Zen master counsels, do *not* speculate.

Instead, return to sender. Do *not* retake the floor, leave the questioner with the floor by saying, "I'm sorry, I didn't follow, would you mind restating the question?" In doing so, *you* take the responsibility for not understanding, rather than pointing out that the questioner asked an unintelligible question.

What will the questioner do?

He or she will rethink the question and then restate it in simpler terms. And you are off the hook. The key here again is the foundation of *Active Listening*: Do *not* answer until you fully comprehend the Roman Column.

Do not answer until you fully comprehend the Roman Column.

Yards After Catch

In North American football, an important measure of success is a statistic called "Yards After Catch." It refers to receivers who catch a pass for a gain of yards and then run for additional yards. Superior receivers are able to add many yards *after* they catch a pass. The not-so-superior receivers, in their desire to become superior, often take their eyes off the ball and start to run *before* they catch the ball. They then fail to make the catch *or* the yards. The play fails.

The analogy applies here. Do not take a step into your answer until your hands are on the ball, until you fully grasp the Roman Column.

You can get the Roman Column on your own with Active Listening, or you can get it by asking the questioner to clarify. Either way, with the key issue firmly in your mind, you are now...and *only* now...finally ready to move forward from the state of suspended animation that we left at the end of Chapter 2 and move forward in the cycle to **Retake the floor**.

CHAPTER 5 Retake the Floor

(Martial Art: Self-Defense)

Become one with the opponent, like an image reflected in the mirror.

Ittosai Sensei Kenpo-Sho
(Teacher Ittosai Sword Manual)
By Kotoda Yahei Toshida [5.1]
(1716)

When your Q&A session moves from **Yield the Floor** to **Retake the Floor**, the shift in dynamics presents another opportunity for you to exercise control. It shifts the energy exchange away from the questioner and back to you.

Let's return our focus to that moment after you have opened the floor to the gentleman in the middle of the back of the room. He has asked his long, rambling question and you, either on your own, or through his own restatement, now fully grasp the Roman Column in his question. Being a results-driven person, you are eager to provide him with an answer, but suppose the gentleman's question was challenging: "Wait a minute! You tell me that your product is going to save us money, and then you give me a sticker shock price that's twice as much as your competition asks! That's outrageous! Where do you get off charging so much?"

Then suppose the answer you give to this very irate person is, "When you consider the total cost of ownership of our solution, you'll see that it will cost you less money in the long run."

You would then be telling your potential buyer that he is wrong. After all, the clear inference in his question was that you are charging too much, and the clear inference in your answer was that you are *not* charging too much.

That irate gentleman would then perceive you as contentious ...similar to the public's perception of Ross Perot when he responded to Al Gore in the NAFTA debate by snarling, "You're lying! You're lying now!" For you, that perception is highly unlikely to induce your potential customer to give you a purchase order.

Another approach, widely considered conventional wisdom, is to repeat the question. However, if immediately after the question, "Where do you get off charging so much?" you were to say, "Where do we get off charging so much?" your echo would validate the inference that you are overcharging. Your potential buyer would then perceive you as having admitted guilt.

What's worse, when you answered, you would most likely start out defensively: "When you consider the total cost of ownership..." In essence, you would be carrying forward a negative balance.

Therefore, when you get a challenging question, do *not* answer and do *not* repeat; *paraphrase* instead.

Paraphrase

The dictionary defines the prefix "para" as *beside; near; alongside,* as in "parallel." This prefix occurs in words such as "paralegal," "paramedical," "parapsychology," and "paramilitary." All of these terms refer to alternate but correlative forms of the root words: legal, medical, psychology, and military. In that same vein, the dictionary defines "paraphrase" as *a restatement of a text or passage in another form or other words, often to clarify meaning.* [5.2]

The intention here is to use the paraphrase during your Q&A session to state the challenging question in another form...to deflect the challenge and to *control* the meaning. This is distinctly different from restating or rephrasing because the prefix "re" means "again." "Again" implies repetition, and repetition implies carrying forward the negative inference latent in the challenging question. A negative statement creates a negative perception. To create a paraphrase of the original question, begin with an interrogative word, such as:

> Use the paraphrase to deflect the challenge and to control the meaning.

- "What...?"
- "Why...?"
- "How...?"
- "Does...?"
- "Can...?"
- "Is...?"

Then conclude your paraphrase with a question mark. These beginning and ending points then serve to bracket the centerpiece of the original question: the Roman Column.

Please note that the paraphrase is *only* a reconfiguration of the original question and *not* a question about the original question. Asking a question *about* a question, as President George H. Bush learned so painfully when he speculated, "Are you suggesting...?" is a tactic doomed to failure.

Answering a question with a question is also a doomed tactic. "Why do you ask?" is an evasive device that has inexplicably gained favor in some quarters of sales training. It is perceived as ducking the issue and produces nothing but frustration and irritation in the asker. Inevitably, irritation in the audience produces failure for the presenter.

A good paraphrase simply incorporates the words of the original question and retains the Roman Column. The paraphrase differs from a question in that the voice drops at the end of the sentence, as opposed to a question in which the voice rises inquisitively.

Now, please look at the original question again: "Wait a minute! You tell me that your product is going to save us money, and then you give me a sticker shock price that's twice as much as your competition asks! That's outrageous! Where do you get off charging so much?"

As in Chapter 4, "Active Listening," the balance of this page is left blank for you to analyze the question "What is the Roman Column?"

If you said "overcharging," "high price," "expensive," or "costly," you would be focusing on the outer wrappings of the knotty ball...the questioner's feeling or emotion *about* the price of your product.

The Roman Column is simply *price*. That is center of the ball, free of any other tangled strands. That, as Sensei Ittosai counsels, is a *reflection of your opponent's image in a mirror.*

Now incorporate the word "price" within a paraphrase.

- What is our *pricing* rationale?
- Why have we chosen this *price* point?
- How did we arrive at the *price*?

Notice that when you strip the charged words, "sticker shock," "twice as much," "outrageous," and "so much," out of the original question, you neutralize the hostility. Then, when you begin your answer, you will only have to address the price itself and not whether it is too high or too low.

> Level the playing field with the paraphrase.

By *becoming one with your opponent* in the paraphrase, you level the playing field. This is the essence of self-defense in the martial arts: By using *agility to counter force*, the engagement then proceeds as a contest between equals.

When you paraphrase in Q&A, you can proceed to answer the question your questioner asked without having to deal with any latent hostility. Your questioner *cannot* help but concur that you have identified the issue, and therefore that person *will not* say...with exasperation, "What I'm *really* asking..." Instead, that person will nod in agreement and release you to move ahead with your answer.

The head nod from your questioner is completely *involuntary*. In my private coaching sessions with my clients, I engage them in an exercise in which they fire tough questions at one another. If the person who is asked the question paraphrases correctly, the person who asked the question invariably nods in agreement. If the paraphrase is wrong, there is no nod. In fact, there is often a frown or a shake of the head. When the paraphrase is correct, the nod *always* happens even though the exercise is a simulation and even though the participants are peers or colleagues and not adversaries.

Let's look at another hostile question: "There are dozens of little start-ups doing exactly what you're doing! Then there are all those big guys, with their entrenched market share. It's a jungle out there, and you're only just getting off the ground! What on earth makes you think that you can survive?"

What is the Roman Column? Decide before you turn the page.

I hope you didn't say "survive." Figure 5.1 shows why not.

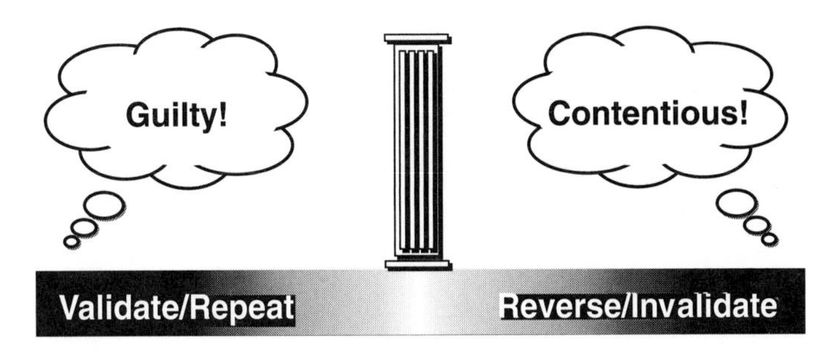

FIGURE 5.1 *Paraphrase positioning.*

Think of the light area in the center of the horizontal bar as the cool zone and the outer dark areas as the danger zones. Your objective is to position the Roman Column in the cool zone.

If you were to *repeat* the challenging question, "What on earth makes me think that we can survive?" you would land in the dark zone on the left because you have *validated* that there is reasonable doubt that you could survive. Your audience would then perceive you as having admitted *guilt*.

If you were to *reverse* the challenging question in your paraphrase, "Why will we succeed in this jungle?" you would land in the dark zone on the right because you have *invalidated* the questioner's concern about your ability to survive. Your audience would then perceive you as having been *contentious*.

The Roman Column is "compete." The paraphrase could be:

- How do we *compete*?
- What is our *competitive* strategy?
- Where are we with our *competitive* strategy?

Find the Roman Column and confine it within the cool zone. Deal with only *how* you compete, not *whether* you can or cannot. Use as few words as possible in your paraphrase. Less is more. Mirror your opponent and neutralize the hostile question.

> Use as few words as possible in your paraphrase.

Here is one more: "You know that this is a male-dominated industry and that most of the buying decisions are made by the buddy system in smoke-filled back rooms. What makes you, a woman, think that you can penetrate that old boy network?"

What is the Roman Column? Decide before you turn the page.

I hope you didn't say "sexism" or "chauvinism." If you did, you would be responding to the value or emotion, the outer wrappings of the knotty ball. The Roman Column is "capability," and the paraphrases are

- What are my *capabilities* to reach decision makers?
- Am I *capable* of reaching decision makers?
- How do my *capabilities* apply to reaching decision makers?

Another version of this hostile question is, "You look like a kid! I doubt that you've been in this business very long. I've been in this industry since before you were born, and now you come in here and tell me how I should run my business. Where do *you* get off telling *me* what to do?"

The Roman Column is the same as above, "capability," not age. The paraphrases are

- What are my *capabilities* to offer you solutions?
- Am I *capable* of offering you solutions?
- How do my *capabilities* apply to our solutions?

All the previous long, rambling, challenging questions can be reduced to three single words: "price," "competition," and "capability." The hostility in each of them is purged by the paraphrase. Also note that all the paraphrases are neutral questions, positioning you to move on to a positive answer. Contrast this approach to the negativity latent in President George H. Bush's words when he retook the floor after Marisa Hall's question.

> *Are you suggesting that if somebody has means that the national debt doesn't affect them?*

Any answer after that would be defensive. Imagine if instead he had paraphrased by saying, "How can a person of means find a cure for those who are less fortunate?"

The answer that would follow that paraphrase would contain an action verb, and be about his ability to provide solutions in response to Marisa Hall's resounding, "How?"

Paraphrasing positions you right in the middle of the cool zone, ready to move forward positively. You can use this very powerful technique to control other types of challenging questions.

Challenging Questions

Negative

"This is the age of mergers. Banks are consolidating. Manufacturing and pharmaceutical companies are joining forces. Everybody's throwing their lot in with others. Instead of going out there and trying to be the Lone Ranger, why don't you throw in your lot with one of the larger companies in your sector? You can either get acquired, merge, or partner."

What is the Roman Column?

The sub-text of the question is this: Why don't you do what the questioner thinks you should do instead of what you just got finished spending your entire presentation telling the audience what you are going to do, which is to go it *alone*, aspiring for market leadership.

The Roman Column is "independence."

If you, as presenter, spend any time dealing with "Why don't you?" questions, you will only invite more negative questions, and you'll be swatting flies all day. Instead, turn the negative into a positive by addressing *only* why you are doing what you said you'd be doing in the presentation. The paraphrase is, "Why are we remaining independent?"

Irrelevant

"How come your logo doesn't have a space between the two words?"

This kind of question usually results in a smile, a snicker, or a frown from the presenter, each of which represents disdain to the questioner. When you're presenting, there is no such thing as an irrelevant question. Every question from every audience member is relevant and appropriate. If they ask it, you must answer it.

> There is no such thing as an irrelevant question. If they ask it, you must answer it.

Inhibit the snicker or frown with the paraphrase, "What's behind our logo design?" or "Why the logo style?"

Multiple Questions

Specifically, *disparate* multiple questions. You will have no difficulty in handling *related* multiple questions such as: "How much did you spend on R&D last year? What percentage of your revenues did that represent? What is your R&D model going forward?" Any financial person could easily handle all three because they are related.

The difficulty comes when one of the multiple questions is from left field, another from right field, and another from the moon. What many presenters do in these circumstances is to dive into an answer for one of them and then lose track of the rest. At that point, the presenter often turns to the questioner and asks, "What was your other question?"

The audience perception: "You *weren't* listening!"

Don't burden yourself with having to remember someone else's right brain, nonlinear data dump. Instead pick only *one* of the questions…the easiest, the hardest, the last, the first, the one that surprised you, or the one that you were expecting. Paraphrase the question, answer it, and then turn back to the person who asked and, in a *declarative* statement say, "You had another question!"

That person will then either repeat the other question, and you can respond with a clear, unencumbered mind; or the questioner might say, "That's all right, you covered it." The latter response is very common in Q&A sessions because most people can't remember their own right brain ramble. Either way, you are off the hook and free to move forward to either answer the second question or move on to another questioner.

Statement

The question that is not a question: "Your new solution appears to be very effective, but you've only just released it. You don't know if it has any kinks. I'd like to see it field-tested before I commit. It's not for us at this time."

If you were trying to land a sale for the early release of your promising new product, you certainly wouldn't want to leave the exchange at that point with no sale. Instead, turn the statement into a question by using the paraphrase, "Why adopt our new product now?" Your answer will then be about why your prospective customer wants to be the first kid on the block to enjoy the many benefits of your promising new product.

Presented Material

The final challenging question is the one about material covered within the presentation. You've probably witnessed this common occurrence: A presenter delivers a very thorough presentation about a new product, only to have a person in the audience ask a question about one of the product's main features already discussed. At an internal company meeting, this usually results in audible groans from other members of the audience. At an external meeting, other audience members, being discrete, stifle their groans and only think them internally.

Presenters, being discrete and hopefully respectful, will also stifle groans but all too often begin their answer by saying, "As I said…" This seemingly innocuous phrase belies impatience with the questioner at best and condescension at worst.

Instead, move directly forward into the answer as if you have never covered the subject. "Absolutely! Our new product performs this function better than any other product on the market!" You are then free to recap the main features of your new product. Resist the temptation, however, to stand on the soap box and repeat the material in as much detail as you did in the presentation. Be succinct!

Avoid back references during Q&A sessions.

Avoiding back references produces three considerable benefits:

- **Reinforcement** of your selling points.
- **Validation**, rather than invalidation, of the questioner.
- **Positive Perception**. Because everyone in the audience heard you cover the material in question and they see you react patiently and positively, they perceive you as a person in control. Cool under fire. Grace under pressure. *Effective Management.*

One important footnote about avoiding back references: In my earlier book, *Presenting to Win: The Art of Telling Your Story*, I advocated back references as a powerful narrative technique to create continuity in any story. However, in the free fire zone of Q&A sessions, where the one-against-many dynamics are in force, the rules change. Therefore, use only forward references.

All the foregoing techniques for handling challenging questions share a least common denominator that brings us full circle back to the martial arts.

The Buffer

By reframing the inbound energy of challenging questions, the paraphrase acts as a Buffer or shock absorber by deflecting the negativity. Like the martial arts, the Buffer is the first line of self-defense. *By becoming one with the opponent*, the Buffer levels the playing field between unequal forces...one presenter and many audience members. Then, after the Buffer discharges the negative energy, the presenter regains balance and moves ahead. The Buffer allows you to

> The Buffer levels the playing field between unequal forces.

- **Neutralize** *hostile* questions.
- **Turn** *negative* questions positive.
- **Treat** *irrelevant* questions the same as any other.
- **Manage** *multiple* questions efficiently.
- **Convert** charged *statements* into questions.
- **Handle** questions about *presented* material with equanimity.

Buffers have a host of other benefits...

- **"I heard you!"** This is the sine qua non of any Q&A session. It tells your questioner...and the rest of the audience...that you listened.
- **Condense**. There is no need to carry forward the right brain nonlinear ramble of your questioner.
- **Thinking Time**. A most valuable asset any time; especially when you are in the line of fire.
- **Verbalize**. Drawn from a rehearsal technique, Verbalization means speaking aloud the actual words in the presentation to crystallize them. By Verbalizing the Buffer, you clarify the Roman Column in your own mind. (You will find a fuller discussion of Verbalization in the section on preparing for Q&A in Chapter 8, "Preparation.")

- **Trigger the Answer**. When your mind is clear on the Roman Column, your answer follows readily.
- **Audibility**. Everyone in the audience hears the question you will answer.

Given all these valuable benefits, you should Buffer all questions, even those that are *not* challenging, such as, "Could you please describe how you plan to market your company in this competitive environment?" However, if you were to paraphrase this question by saying, "Could I describe how we're planning to market our company in this competitive environment?" you would sound awkward. Another option is to Buffer with *Key Words*.

Key Words

In the case of non-challenging direct questions you can shift to a shorter Buffer, using the Key Word or Words that identify the Roman Column and roll those words into your answer. An example would be, "Our marketing plan includes…" Or you can use the Key Words as an *echo*…"Our marketing plan?" and then proceed with your answer.

Use the Key Word Buffer and roll into your answer.

You also can use this Key Words Buffer technique for tough questions, like the opening salvo in this chapter: "Wait a minute! You tell me that your product is going to save us money, and then you give me a sticker shock price that's twice as much as your competition asks! That's outrageous! Where do you get off charging so much?"

The *Key Word* Buffer is, "Our *pricing* rationale is…"

Or the second round salvo: "There are dozens of little start-ups doing exactly what you're doing! Then there are all those big guys with their entrenched market share. It's a jungle out there, and you're only just getting off the ground! What on earth makes you think that you can survive?"

The *Key Word* Buffer is, "The way we will *compete* is..."

Or the third round salvo: "You know that this is a male-dominated industry and that most of the buying decisions are made by the buddy system in smoke-filled back rooms. What makes you, a woman, think that you can penetrate that old boy network?"

The *Key Word* Buffer is, "My *capabilities* include..."

Now you have two types of Buffer. One is the paraphrase that restates the question, and the other is to state the Key Words and then continue on into your answer. However, some presenters are not content with one Buffer. They feel the need to put a Buffer in front of the Buffer, otherwise known as a *Double Buffer.* In the section that follows, you'll find...and most likely recognize...a collection of the most common Double Buffers used in Q&A sessions, all of which are useless fillers at the very least or counterproductive at the worst.

The Double Buffer

The most common Double Buffer is

- *"The question is..."*

It's all right to use this once. It's all right to use it twice. It's all right to use it three times. But if you use it before every paraphrase, it sounds as if you're stalling for time.

Two other common stalls for time are

- *"That was a good question."*
- *"I'm glad you asked that."*

Presenters often resort to either of these Double Buffers as a delaying tactic in reaction to a challenging question that was actually *not* good, nor are they glad to have been asked it.

On the other hand, suppose an audience member *did* ask you a question that was good for you, such as, "All these new features in your product should allow us to get our product to market faster, right?" You could then gleefully use *both* Double Buffers: "That was a good question! I'm glad you asked that!" You could then go on to extol the virtues of your new product features.

But then suppose the next audience member asked you, "Yes, but why do you charge so much for your product?" You would hardly say, "That was a *bad* question! I'm *not* glad you asked that!" That would be judging and favoring one audience member over the other.

Another common Double Buffer is

- *"What you're really asking..."*

The implication of this phrase is that the questioner isn't capable of formulating the question correctly and that the presenter will charitably reformulate it...an insult to the audience member.

And another common Double Buffer is

- *"If I understand your question..."*

The implication of this Double Buffer is the fatal message, "I wasn't listening." And the final common Double Buffer is

- *"The issue/concern is..."*

If you use the word "concern" or "issue" upon retaking the floor, you will be confirming that there is a concern or an issue between you and your audience. Worse still, you will begin your answer carrying forward a negative balance.

Delete all the Double Buffers listed here from your vocabulary. If you want to use Double Buffers, insert the word "you."

The Power of "You"

Insert a "you" in your Double Buffer before your paraphrase.

- "You're asking..."
- "You'd like to know..."
- "Your question is..."

Contrast the first Double Buffer in this section with the last:

- "The question is..."
- "Your question is..."

The difference is one word, "you," one of the most powerful in all human communication. A Google search of the Internet abounds with citations of a Yale University study of the most persuasive words in the English language in which "you" leads the list, ahead of "love" and "money." A simpler proof of the power of "you" is that it is synonymous with a person's name. Further validation comes from the branding slogans of some of the world's most successful corporations:

- Are *you* ready? (Cisco Systems)
- *You*r potential, Our passion (Microsoft Corporation)
- Have it your way (Burger King)

Moreover, saying "you" establishes a direct interpersonal connection between you and your questioner. It creates Eye Connect between you and your questioner. *Eye Connect* is a more specific term than the conventional "eye contact," which is usually done as a sweeping movement. *Eye Connect* means that you look at a person in your audience until you see him or her look back at you...until you feel the click of engagement.

Here is why *Eye Connect* is important: If you were to look at your questioner during a long rambling question and then use the first Double Buffer listed earlier, "The question is..." you would most likely turn to address the rest of the audience. This would abruptly break your *Eye Connect* with your questioner and make that person feel rudely abandoned.

If instead you were to use the second Double Buffer, "Your question is…" you would then remain in *Eye Connect* with your questioner and make that person feel attended. Moreover, you would then see how that person reacts to your Buffer. A frown would indicate that you didn't get it right, and a head nod would indicate that you did. When you get the head nod from your questioner, and *only* after you get the head nod, are you free to begin your answer.

Only after you get the head nod are you free to begin your answer.

The head nod is the equivalent of Marisa Hall's, "Well, yeah, uh-huh." The head nod is the ultimate benefit because it sends the message, "You heard me!" And remember, the head nod in response to an accurate Buffer is *involuntary*.

All the foregoing control measures, starting with the moment you retake the floor and continuing up to the moment when you are ready to provide an answer, can be summarized in what is known as the *Triple Fail-Safe*.

The Triple Fail-Safe

First Fail-Safe. Retake the floor *only* after you have a complete grasp of the Roman Column in the question. This is the equivalent of successful football receivers who run for Yards After Catch *only* after they have a complete grasp of the ball. If you do not completely grasp the Roman Column, do not take a step forward. Instead, follow the same instructions the U.S. Postal Service stamps on mail with unclear addresses: *Return to Sender*. Return the floor to the questioner by taking responsibility and saying,

"I'm sorry, I didn't follow; would you mind restating the question?"

Second Fail-Safe. If you are certain that you have grasped the Roman Column, use the key word in your Buffer. During your Buffer, make *Eye Connect* with the questioner until you see that person's head nod, indicating that you have identified the Roman Column correctly. Move forward into your answer only after you see the head nod.

Third Fail-Safe. If, despite your best efforts, you get a frown instead of a nod, do not move forward into the answer. Instead, *Return to Sender* by saying, "I'm sorry, I didn't follow, would you mind restating the question?"

These three Fail-Safes, depicted in Figure 5.2, are check points that will keep you from rushing into the wrong answer. You will also avoid the dreaded, "You're *not* listening!" perception or its close cousins, "That's not what I asked!" and "What I'm *really* asking…"

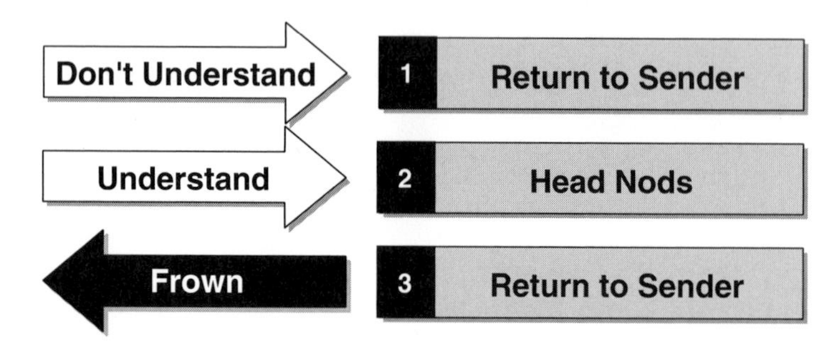

▲ **FIGURE 5.2** *The Triple Fail-Safe.*

Even with the Triple Fail-Safe, there is the possibility that, because the Roman Column straddles two related issues, you might not fully address both of them in your answer. At that point, the worst that can happen is that the questioner will ask you a follow-on question, "Yes, but what I'd also like to know is…" which is a lot milder than the dreaded, "You're *not* listening!" reaction.

Figure 5.3 is a graphical summary of this entire chapter: A question and an answer can be bridged by any of three Buffer options:

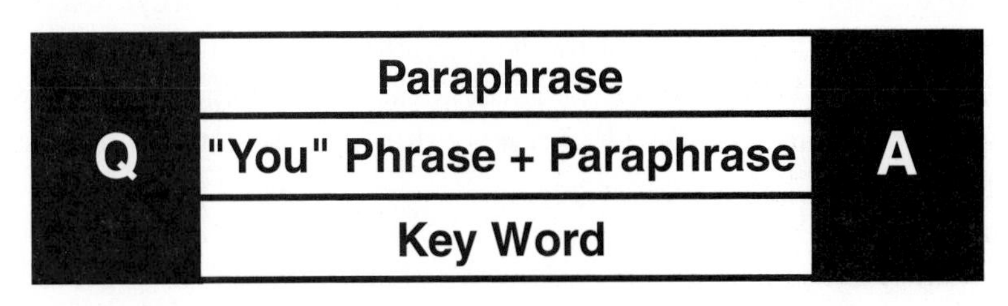

FIGURE 5.3 *Buffer summary.*

Paraphrase. A simple interrogative question.

- "Why have we chosen this *price* point?"
- "What are my *capabilities* to reach decision makers?"
- "How do we *compete*?"

A "you" phrase before the paraphrase.

- "You're asking, 'Why have we chosen this *price* point?'"
- "Your question is, 'What are my *capabilities* to reach decision makers?'"
- "You'd like to know how we *compete*."

Key Words.

- "Our *pricing* is based on…"
- "My *capabilities* include…"
- "The way we *compete* is…"

The first two Buffer options, the paraphrase and the paraphrase preceded by a "you" phrase, buy you thinking time. However, if you use these Buffers too often in your session, you will sound stilted…particularly with the "you" phrase. Although "you" has the many benefits as discussed, it can become too much of a good thing. Starting *every* Buffer with "you" will make you sound like a hoot owl.

Key Words, the third Buffer option, allows you no thinking time at all. You must have the ball firmly in your hands before you take a single step. Make sure that the Roman Column is crystal clear in your mind when you utter the first word. However, when you respond without a moment's hesitation, with the Key Word embedded in your answer, you will appear very sharp, very much in control. The Key Word option is the most advanced form of Buffering.

An outstanding role model of Key Word Buffering is Colin Powell, one of the best presenters or speakers ever to stand at a podium. As the U.S. Secretary of State, Mr. Powell held a press conference for foreign journalists on April 15, 2003, at the Foreign Press Center in Washington, D.C., shortly after the start of the Iraq War (Figure 5.4).

▲ **FIGURE 5.4** *Colin Powell holds a press conference.*

During the session, Mr. Powell fielded 11 questions. Never once did he paraphrase or use a Double Buffer. In every case, he began his answer with the Key Word or Words inherent in the reporters' questions. Consider his challenge: Most of the foreign journalists spoke English as a second language, and so they phrased their questions with syntax and accents that were not native to Mr. Powell. Moreover, as professional journalists, they all tried to cram in multiple questions when their turns came.

In the following section from the transcript of the conference, we'll look at several of the reporters' questions and then how, in each instance, Mr. Powell promptly retook the floor with only the Key Word Buffer to start his answer. Although his thorough answers continued well beyond his Key Word Buffer, in the interest of illustrating this powerful technique, we will examine only the front end of his answers...the inflection point at which he retook the floor and exercised control.

Mr. Powell made a brief opening statement and then opened the floor.

> *I would be delighted to take your questions.*

The first question came from a Russian man.

> *As the chief foreign policy advisor to U.S. President, do you think the UN is still relevant and important from the point of view of prevention of military conflicts, not only humanitarian assistance, and do you think the organization needs to be reformed?*

What is the Key Word? Certainly not the last word, "reformed." If Powell were to deal with that issue, he would land in the dark danger zone on the left of Figure 5.1 because he would be *validating* the reporter's assertion that the United Nations is irrelevant and in need of reform. Any answer would then be an uphill fight to justify the U.N., which was the very opposite of the United States' stated supportive policy. Instead, the Secretary's first words upon retaking the floor were:

> *The UN remains an important organization.*

These Key Words served as a neutralizing Buffer that allowed Powell to go on to offer supporting evidence.

> *The President and other leaders in the coalition...Prime Minister Blair, President Aznar, Prime Minister Berlusconi and many others, Prime Minister Howard of Australia...have all indicated that they believe the UN has a role to play as we go forward in the reconstruction and the rebuilding of Iraq.*

His answer continued beyond this point, but let's move on to another question, this one from an Egyptian woman.

> *Thank you. Sir, the Israelis said that they presented to you their modification on the roadmap. Have you received anything from the other side, from the Palestinians? And is it still open for change? You have told us before that it is not negotiable. And now on the settlements, on the settlements, as part of the roadmap, eh?*

She was clearly rambling, so Powell tried to get her to clarify.

> *The what?*

She tried to explain herself.

> *On the settlements, which is part of the roadmap, we see the Israelis are...the activities of building settlements is really very high. We saw it on television. We saw reports...*

He tried to get her to finish by interjecting.

> *Thank you.*

She continued,

> *So what is your remarks on the settlements?*

What is the Key Word? Certainly not her last words, "the settlements." If Powell were to deal with that issue, he would he would again land in the dark danger zone on the left of Figure 5.1 because he would be *validating* the reporter's concern with an obstacle to the United States-sponsored peace efforts. Any answer would then focus on only a subordinate aspect of the U.S.'s larger initiative: the roadmap. Instead, his first words upon retaking the floor were:

With respect to the roadmap...

By using "the roadmap" as the Key Words rather than "the settlements," Powell created a neutralizing Buffer. This allowed him to move on to a substantive rather than defensive statement.

...the roadmap will be released to the parties after Mr. Abu Mazen is confirmed, and it will be the roadmap draft that was finished last December.

He continued his answer to her, but let's proceed to another question, this one from a Lebanese journalist.

Mr. Secretary, a lot of fears have been made about who is next. And some people believed to be close with the administration said that the regimes backing Cairo and in Saudi Arabia should be nervous right now. How do you address that point? And does the U.S. has a plan to spread a set of values at gunpoint, in your view, at this point?

"A plan to spread a set of values at gunpoint..." This question accused the United States of acting as a villainous bully, and Powell could not give credence to this charge! When he retook the floor, he immediately countered the accusation by applying the noted anti-drug slogan, "Just say, 'No!'"

No, of course not.

Neither Colin Powell, nor you, nor *any* presenter is under *any* obligation to respond to an accusation that is untrue in *any* other way than with a complete refutation. If you are attacked with a question that contains or implies an inaccuracy, do as Colin Powell did; skip the Buffer and come back immediately with a rebuttal.

No presenter is under any obligation to respond to an accusation that is untrue in any other way than with a complete refutation.

After his rebuttal, Powell went on to support his position:

> *The President has spoken clearly about this, as recently as two days ago, over the weekend. We have concerns about Syria. We have let Syria know of our concerns. We also have concerns about some of the policies of Iran. We have made the Iranians fully aware of our concerns.*

He concluded with a firm restatement of his rebuttal.

> *But there is no list.*

This exchange was a variation of the common, "When did you stopping beating your wife?" question. The correct response to that implied charge is, "I never started beating my wife." Counter the false charge on the spot. Stop it in its tracks. Just say, "No!"

Colin Powell then had another accusation fired at him by a Mexican reporter, who asked,

> *Mr. Secretary, I have a question on Cuba. Can you give us an assessment of what is your advice to the countries that are near to both in terms of the human rights situation in Cuba, especially to Mexico that has been too close to the Cuban Government? And a quick second question. There is some countries that are calling the United States the "police of the world." Do you agree with that?*

"The police of the world..." Here was another question which accused the United States of acting as a villainous bully! It was another variation of "When did you stop beating your wife?" Here again, Powell could not give any credence to this charge in his reply. However, because it was a double question, he fielded them in order, with Cuba first.

> *First of all, with respect to Cuba, it has always had a horrible human rights record. And rather than improving as we go into the 21st century, it's getting worse.*

Then, after a few supporting points about Cuba, he countered the accusation by just saying "No!"

> *With respect to the United States being the policemen of the world, we do not seek war, we do not look for wars, we do not need wars, we do not want wars.*

So it went with every other question in the press conference. Powell listened carefully and answered as each of the reporters challenged him with multiple questions, until he came to an Australian reporter.

> *Mr. Secretary, there seems to be some hopeful sounds coming out of your administration and North Korea on a settlement there. Do you think that there is likely to be a meeting soon between the administration and North Korea? And what sort of forum do you expect to attend? And how much do you think this is a flow-on from what happened in Iraq?*

Powell broke into a big grin.

> *Very good. You're trying to get it all at once, aren't you? [5.3]*

Powell then did go on to provide an answer about U.S. relations with North Korea. As with all the others, he began his answer with the Key Word Buffer and then went on to state his position consistent with United States policy.

In each case, the Key Word Buffer technique provides the major benefits of the Buffer:

- Identifies the Roman Column
- Condenses the ramble
- Levels the playing field
- Tees up the answer

...all of which tees you up to learn how to answer in the next chapter.

Chapter 6: Provide the Answer

(Martial Art: Balance)

The Yin and Yang are two interlocking complementaries...Yin can represent anything in the universe as negativeness...Yang can represent anything as positiveness...Yin/Yang is one inseparable force of one unceasing interplay of movement.

Bruce Lee (1940-1973) [6.1]

Here we are five chapters into this book, and we have yet to touch on how to provide an answer to tough questions. This delay is fully intentional. Results-driven people, like you, tend to rush to answer too soon, which can produce the negative results that befell President George H. Bush. During the delay, we've established the two vital prerequisites to the answer:

- Listen for the Roman Column
- Confirm the Roman Column to the questioner in the Buffer

Conventional approaches to Q&A skills via public relations advisors, investor relations counselors, and media trainers merely list the potential questions and provide another parallel list of appropriate answers. This is a straightforward cause and effect or problem/solution approach, and is as necessary as balance is in the martial arts, but it skips the two critical prerequisites just noted. It is only when you have fulfilled these two vital requirements that are you ready to move on to the final inflection point in the Q&A scenario...the answer.

Quid Pro Quo

The correct way to answer any question is governed by one overarching principal that goes back to the way to handle an irrelevant question: *If they ask it, you must answer it.* The same applies to *all* questions. After you open the floor...and yourself...to questions, your obligation is to respond. Other than questions to which you do not know the answer, you must reply to *any* question from *any* audience member. As in the martial arts, you must counterbalance one force with another; provide the complementary positive for the negative in the tough question: provide the Yang for the Yin.

> You must reply to any question from any audience member.

Furthermore, your answer must address the Roman Column directly. Anything less will result in the "That's *not* what I asked!" or "What I'm *really* asking..." reaction, which is synonymous with "You weren't listening!" The George H. Bush/Marisa Hall effect.

Any attempt to duck the issue in the answer will appear to be defensive or evasive. Remember how defensive Bob Newhart appeared when he replied to Ruth Corley's question, "So your answer is 'No,'" by stammering, "No, no my answer is not 'No.'" Remember how evasive Trent Lott appeared when he explained his admiration for the segregationist, Strom Thurmond, by attributing it to everything from law and order to fiscal responsibility...everything but segregation.

Bob Newhart's stammer was for comic effect, but Trent Lott's dodge produced a disastrous effect. The television anchorman pursued Lott to admit that he knew Thurmond was a segregationist, until Lott finally conceded. The lesson here is the same as in the martial arts: Meet the key issue in the Roman Column head on. Remember, too, the absolute requirement for truth: *Every answer you give to every question you get must always be honest and straightforward.*

Every answer you give to every question you get must always be honest and straightforward.

Manage the Answer

But meet the issue only head on. Resist the common temptation to introduce new, tangential information during your Q&A session. Far too many presenters veer off into another presentation *after* their presentation. Keep in mind that the only purpose in opening the floor to questions is to clarify the material *within* your presentation or speech. Operate under the premise that you have covered all of your material thoroughly and that the Q&A period is a courtesy to the audience to provide elaboration for them upon request.

Under that same assumption, keep all your answers succinct. Resist the other common temptation to launch into oratory or to wax eloquent. A simple rule of thumb that will serve for most questions in most settings is to keep your answers to a maximum of 60 seconds.

Anticipate

In advance of placing yourself in the line of fire, compile a list of the most challenging questions you might be asked. Compile only the questions and not the answers. Seek input for your list from as many resources as possible...your colleagues, your customers, your partners, your consultants and, if you can, even your competitors. When politicians prepare for debates, they get stand-ins for their opponents for their practice sessions. The next chapter will cover practice and preparation in greater detail, but for now, be your own stand-in.

You know more about your own business premise than anyone else. Assemble the go-for-the-jugular questions, assume the worst-case scenarios. After your list is compiled, however, look it over carefully. You'll discover that, even if there are 100 tough questions, they all fall into groups of only a handful of red flag issues. You may also be surprised to discover that those red flag issues are the same in almost every industry. In my private practice, Power Presentations, Ltd., I consult for companies in Information Technology, Biotechnology, Manufacturing, Real Estate, Retail, Restaurants, and even in the not-for-profit sector, and they all share the same universal red flag issues.

Recognize the Universal Issues

- **Management**. Do you have the right people? Is your team complete?
- **Competition**. How will you meet and beat the competition?
- **Growth**. How will you produce hockey stick results?
- **Price/Cost**. What is your pricing rationale?
- **Contingencies**. What will you do if…?
- **Timing**. What's taken you so long? Why don't you wait?
- **Problems**. Questions about problems are usually phrased as, "What keeps you up at night?" Answer that question candidly, stating what does concern you, but then immediately follow with the actions you are taking to solve those problems.
- **Intellectual Property**. As with problem questions, be candid about any litigious situations, but then immediately follow with the steps you are taking to protect and defend your ideas, or defer to legal counsel.

When you have identified these red flag issues as they relate to your business, develop a *position statement* for each of them. Craft this statement as if you were writing a press release for the media. This will take discussion and consultation with your key colleagues. When you have arrived at a consensus, it is merely a matter of aligning the variation of the position statement with the variation of the issue in the challenging question. Do all your positioning during your *preparation* and not your *presentation*. Do all your thinking offline and not on your feet.

Develop a position statement for each red flag issue.

How to Handle Special Questions

Several special types of questions require special handling.

Tangential. In the previous chapter, you saw that there is no such thing as an irrelevant question such as, "How come your logo doesn't have a space between the two words?" Such a question is, however, tangential and, as with *any* question, deserves an answer. Therefore, once you Buffer to keep from snickering or frowning at the questioner, you can either answer it directly, "We chose that as our branding style," or take it offline, "There are several reasons that I can share with you after the presentation."

Inaccurate. This is the familiar, "When did you stop beating your wife?" question, a close cousin of the overstated accusations hurled at Colin Powell…that "The U.S. has a plan to spread a set of values at gunpoint," and was acting as "The police of the world." Counter such false charges with the advice from the previous chapter: *Neither Colin Powell, nor you, nor any presenter is under any obligation to respond to an accusation that is untrue in any other way than with a complete refutation.* Just say, "No!"

Unknown. No audience member can reasonably expect you to be a walking encyclopedia, so if you do not know the answer to a question, particularly if it is about some minute detail, admit it to your questioner, but promise to get the answer to that person later. To demonstrate your intent, ask for a business card.

However, if the question is spot on to a central issue to your cause, you must respond directly and cannot duck it, or you will appear to be evasive.

President George W. Bush was confronted with such a situation on April 13, 2004. In the midst of a rare prime-time press conference about the controversial war in Iraq, a reporter asked:

> *In the last campaign, you were asked a question about the biggest mistake you'd made in your life, and you used to like to joke that it was trading Sammy Sosa. You've looked back before 9/11 for what mistakes might have been made. After 9/11, what would your biggest mistake be, would you say, and what lessons have you learned from it?*

President Bush replied:

> *I wish you would have given me this written question ahead of time, so I could plan for it. John, I'm sure historians will look back and say, gosh, he could have done it better this way, or that way. You know, I just—I'm sure something will pop into my head here in the midst of this press conference, with all the pressure of trying to come up with an answer, but it hadn't yet.*

He went on to reiterate the rationale for going into Afghanistan and Iraq and then concluded his answer with these words

> *I hope I—I don't want to sound like I've made no mistakes. I'm confident I have. I just haven't—you just put me under the spot here, and maybe I'm not as quick on my feet as I should be in coming up with one. [6.2]*

His response drew a great deal of attention in the media as being evasive. True to form, the media pursued the subject. Four months later, during an interview with *The New York Times,* a reporter asked the President:

> *At your last big press conference, you said that you couldn't think of any mistakes you had made. It's been about three or four months. Can you think of any now? It's been a long time.*

This time, President Bush was able to joke about a mistake:

> *You mean other than having this interview?*

At another point in the interview, he even acknowledged a perfectly understandable mistake.

It's a miscalculation of the—what the conditions would be like after a swift victory, because we never dreamt it would be that swift. [6.3]

The subject was still alive two months later when President Bush met Senator Kerry to debate in a town-hall format at Washington University, St. Louis, Missouri. One of the audience members, Linda Grabel, asked:

President Bush, during the last four years, you have made thousands of decisions that have affected millions of lives. Please give three instances in which you came to realize you had made a wrong decision, and what you did to correct it. Thank you.

President Bush answered:

I have made a lot of decisions, and some of them little, like appointments to boards you never heard of, and some of them big. And in a war, there's a lot of—there's a lot of tactical decisions that historians will look back and say: He shouldn't have done that. He shouldn't have made that decision. And I'll take responsibility for them. I'm human. But on the big questions, about whether or not we should have gone into Afghanistan, the big question about whether we should have removed somebody in Iraq, I'll stand by those decisions, because I think they're right.

That's really what you're—when they ask about the mistakes, that's what they're talking about. They're trying to say, "Did you make a mistake going into Iraq?" And the answer is, "Absolutely not." It was the right decision.

This time, the President provided quid pro quo to Linda Grabel's challenge by standing by his decision. He went on to further support his actions and then concluded his answer:

Now, you asked what mistakes. I made some mistakes in appointing people, but I'm not going to name them. I don't

> *want to hurt their feelings on national TV. But history will look back, and I'm fully prepared to accept any mistakes that history judges to my administration, because the president makes the decisions, the president has to take the responsibility. [6.4]*

The lesson here is that you *must* answer tough questions *directly*. You can do it lightly, with self-deprecating humor, be frank and fess up, or stand your ground, but you must address the issues that are prominent in the minds of your audience. Remember David Bellet's words from the Introduction: "What I look for is whether the presenter has thought about the question, been candid, thorough, and direct." (*Note:* You'll see a more extensive discussion of all three of the 2004 presidential debates in Chapter 9, "The Art of War.")

> You must answer tough questions directly.

Confidential. If you get a question about classified or restricted material, and you say, "I'm not at liberty to reveal that," you will sound evasive. You will sound even more so if you say, "If I told you I'd have to kill you!"

Instead, provide a reason for your confidentiality. Attribute it to company policy, security, competitive data, legality, or privacy, and do it positively rather negatively. Rather than say, "We don't provide such confidential information," say, "It's our policy to provide only information previously mentioned in our press releases." In the Introduction, Bill Clinton's response to a question about Monica Lewinsky was, "At this minute, I am going to stick with my position and not comment," attributing his confidentiality to implied legal reasons.

Senator John F. Kerry ran afoul of a confidential question during his 2004 quest for the presidency. Early in his campaign, Kerry made the claim that foreign leaders backed his candidacy. Then, on March 14, at a town-hall meeting in Pennsylvania, one man repeatedly asked the senator to identify which leaders, and Kerry repeatedly refused. The man continued to badger Kerry until in exasperation he blurted,

> *That's not your business! It's mine!*

The immediate perception was that Kerry had something to hide. Later, in a calmer moment, Kerry explained:

> *No leader would obviously share a conversation if I started listing them. [6.5]*

The lesson for John Kerry is that he learned to attribute his reluctance to confidentiality rather than to prying. The lesson for you is this: If you cannot provide an answer, provide a valid reason.

If you cannot provide an answer, provide a valid reason.

Speculative. If you get a question that requires a forward looking statement, such as, "When will you be profitable?" Don't forecast and attribute your restraint to company policy.

Guilty as charged. Suppose you were to get a question concerning an issue about which you or your company are guilty as charged. For instance, if your start-up company is entering a sector dominated by a larger company, and you get the question from the previous chapter, "There are dozens of little start-ups doing exactly what you're doing! Then there all those big guys, with their entrenched market share. It's a jungle out there, and you're only just getting off the ground! What on earth makes you think that you can survive?"

Or if you were President George H. Bush, and Marisa Hall asked, "How has the national debt personally affected each of your lives? And if it hasn't, how can you honestly find a cure for the economic problems of the common people if you have no experience in what's ailing them?"

In each case, the underlying issue is that the question is true. Start-ups *do* have a difficult challenge, and a millionaire such as

George H. Bush does *not* have personal experience in what is ailing people caught in an economic downturn.

However, neither you nor the president of the United States has to plead guilty to the charge and surrender.

Guilty as Charged Questions

Here is what President Bush actually said in response to Marisa Hall's question:

> *Are you suggesting that if somebody has means that the national debt doesn't affect them? [6.6]*

Any answer after that kind of negative statement would be defensive. Here is what he might have done instead:

- **Buffer**. "How can a person of means…" using the same term he used before he sputtered and gave up, "…find a cure…" restating Marisa Hall's own words, "…for those who are less fortunate?"
- **Agree**. "You're absolutely right," then, using more of her words, "I don't make mortgage payments or car payments…"
- **"But…"** Don't agree too long. Step on the brakes with a loud, "But…" (There is a proverbial story about the 1000-word sentence in which the 998th word is "but," that invalidates all the previous 997 words.) The "but" either diminishes or invalidates any admission of guilt. After the "But…" pivot and make a sharp U-turn. "… that doesn't mean that I don't care."
- **Evidence**. "As a matter of fact, young woman, I care so much that during my first administration, I initiated an X, and a Y, and a Z program to help people who are less fortunate than I am."
- **Call to action and offer the benefit**. "So if you'll only elect me to a second term, I'll initiate even more such programs."

Just think...if President Bush had followed this sequence, the world might never have heard of Monica Lewinsky.

Imagine if a start-up company CEO challenged about "the jungle out there" were to follow the same sequence.

- **Buffer**. "How will we compete?"
- **Agree**. "You're absolutely right; it is a jungle out there."
- **"But..."** Don't agree too long. Step on the brakes with a loud "But..." Then pivot and make a sharp U-turn. "... that doesn't mean that there isn't room for a new entrant."
- **Evidence**. "Those large companies are top heavy and have multiple interests, while our agility and sole focus have netted us fifteen major customers in our first year of operation."
- **Call to action and offer the benefit**. "So we're confident that we can not only compete effectively, but will succeed in this market."

In this powerful sequence, the presenter transmits a dynamic wave that has multiple benefits:

- Identifies the Roman Column
- Strips out the negativity
- Acknowledges the questioner's concerns
- Dispels the questioner's concerns
- Addresses the questioner's concerns
- Concludes confidently

That confident conclusion comes from the last step, which is the presenter's call to action and the benefit to the audience. These terms also can be stated as *Point B* and *WIIFY*.

Point B and WIIFY

These are terms I introduced in my previous book, *Presenting to Win: The Art of Telling Your Story*.

- **Point B**. The audience in *any* communication situation begins at Point A, *un*informed, *un*convinced, and *not* ready to act. It is the presenter's objective, goal, or message to move the audience to Point B: *well* informed, *thoroughly* convinced, and *completely* ready to act. This dynamic shift is the fine art of persuasion. Point B is the call to action.

- **WIIFY**. An acronym (pronounced "whiffy") that stands for, "What's in it for *you*?" based on the more common axiom, "What's in it for *me*?" The shift from "me" to "you" is deliberate, not just to utilize the power of the "you" word, but to shift the focus from the presenter to the audience. This shift states the benefit to the audience and gives the audience a reason to move from Point A to Point B. People need a reason to act, and it must be their reason, not yours. The WIIFY is the reason.

A simple way to look at Point B is *what* you want your audience to do, and the WIIFY is *why* they should do it.

> Point B is what you want your audience to do, and the WIIFY is why they should do it.

Topspin

In Q&A sessions, stating Point B or a WIIFY at the end of the answer to a challenging question produces a strong and confident conclusion. Taken together, this strong ending is called *Topspin*, from the tennis term for a stroke that hits the ball high, forcing it to bounce sharply and making it difficult for the opponent to return. Topspin in tennis is a power stroke that gives a player a winning advantage. Topspin in Q&A is a power stroke that gives a presenter or speaker a winning advantage. (See Figure 6.1.)

> Topspin in Q&A is a power stroke that gives a presenter or speaker a winning advantage.

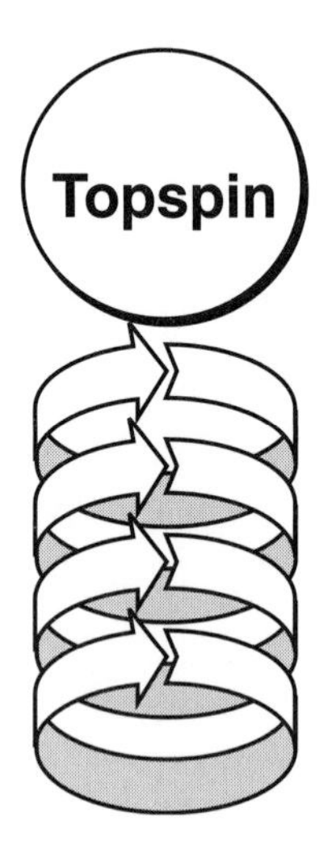

▲ **FIGURE 6.1** *Topspin.*

Please note that the icon for Topspin contains *multiple* upward swirling arrows; this is meant to encourage you to add *multiple* variations of your Point B, your call to action, and the WIIFY, the reason for your audience to act. After you have gone through the ordeal of listening, Buffering and answering tough questions, you have earned the right to promote your own cause and its benefits. Swirl your arrows upward. In your rehearsals, prompt yourself and/or your colleagues by using the gesture I use to coach my private clients: Point your forefinger skyward and twirl it...Topspin.

You will learn more about how to add Topspin to your answers in the next chapter, but first an important footnote to the technique of agreeing with guilty-as-charged questions.

Media Sound Bites

Presenters and speakers often deliver their stories to journalists who record the exchange on paper or computer or video or audio tape. At that point, the presenter cedes control to the journalist, who is free to reproduce and publish or broadcast any part of the interview out of context.

Therefore, if President George H. Bush had said to a reporter:

> *You're absolutely right. I don't make mortgage payments or car payments.*

The reporter could then publish or broadcast those words isolated from the rest of the text and follow it with a commentary, "President Bush admits he doesn't understand the impact of the economy."

Or if a CEO said to a reporter:

> *You're absolutely right; it is a jungle out there.*

The reporter could then publish or broadcast those words isolated from the rest of the text and follow it with a commentary, "CEO admits major obstacles to success."

Therefore, whenever you engage in a media exchange, do not agree with guilty-as-charged questions. Instead, immediately counter the charge:

> *I am fully capable of helping people impacted by the economy.*
>
> *I am fully confident that we can succeed in a competitive environment.*

Or, if you want to acknowledge the guilty charge, downplay it as a subordinate clause before your counterstatement.

While I don't make mortgage payments and car payments myself, I can still use the power of my office to help people impacted by the economy.

While the competitive arena is a jungle, I am fully confident that we can succeed.

Note that each counterstatement is punctuated with Topspin: "help people" is a WIIFY, and "we can succeed," is a Point B. In the next chapter, you will learn more about this powerful technique by seeing it in action in mission-critical situations.

CHAPTER

Topspin in Action

(Martial Art: Agility)

Guard against your opponent, wait for his move then immediately switch to the offensive.

Hei-Ho-Kaden-Sho
(Hereditary Manual of the Martial Arts)
By Yagyu Tajimanokami Munenori [7.1]
(1571–1647)

Topspin presents further parallels with the martial arts. It moves the combative exchange from the defensive, deflecting the challenger's negative energy, to the offensive, asserting influence over the challenger. However, exerting that influence is not easy; it requires the presenter to overcome opposing natural instincts. Human beings, when faced with danger, either try to protect themselves or escape the conflict: the classic Fight or Flight reaction.

Most presenters, when faced with challenging questions, respond with either the Fight reaction: a terse defensive or evasive answer; or the Flight reaction, a short effective answer and then a rush to move on to the next question. For presenters to stand their ground and add another sentence or two of Topspin requires an act of extreme will. To Topspin *well* requires a skill of extreme mental dexterity.

Just how difficult this can be is illustrated in the field of politics where candidates must stand toe-to-toe with their opponents in debate, in front of the public in open forums, or exposed to the press in the glare of the media spotlight.

Michael Dukakis Misses a Free Kick

Massachusetts Governor Michael Dukakis had his big moment in the media spotlight during the U.S. presidential election of 1988. As the Democratic candidate, Dukakis had twice debated George H. Bush, the incumbent vice president, but was still behind in the polls. Eager to have another chance, he accepted an offer from ABC television for a joint appearance 13 days before the election on its *Nightline* series. The Bush team declined the offer, and Dukakis, liberated from television's equal time requirements or a rebuttal from his opponent, had the equivalent of what in football is known as a free kick.

However, during the live broadcast, when host Ted Koppel asked Dukakis a challenging question about his ability to lead the country, he replied:

> *I guess the thing that concerns me the most is that I've found it very difficult to give people in this country a real sense of who the real Mike Dukakis is. Who I am, what I care about. And the kind of deep commitment I have to people in the communities and to this country, and why I'm running for presidency. You know, I've... people have said, well, I'm kind of cool. Don't have enough passion and so on. People who know me know just how deeply I feel about this country, and about our future, and about public service. And why I've been in public service for 25 years. But it's very difficult to convey that. [7.2]*

By concluding his answer with "It's very difficult to convey that," Michael Dukakis spiraled downward, ending negatively. Imagine if the governor had heeded the advice of Master Munenori and *immediately switched to the offensive* by saying instead,

> *"People have said, well, I'm kind of cool. Don't have enough passion and so on, but people who know me, know just how deeply I feel about this country, and about our future, and about public service. And why I've been in public service for 25 years. And if they knew the kind of deep commitment I have to people in the communities and to this country, they would vote for me for the presidency."*

"Vote for me for the presidency," would have been Michael Dukakis' Topspin, his Point B, in his campaign against George H. Bush.

Imagine if George H. Bush, in his 1992 debate with Bill Clinton, had concluded his answer to Marisa Hall by saying, "So if you'll only elect me to a second term, I'll initiate even more such programs." This would have been George H. Bush's Point B as well as Marisa Hall's WIIFY.

Eight years later, George H. Bush's son, George W. Bush, ran for the presidency and was confronted with the challenge of employing Topspin effectively.

The Evolution of George W. Bush

During the U.S. presidential election of 2000, then Governor of Texas George W. Bush's chronic difficulty with the English language made him the constant butt of jokes in the media and the endless target of late-night comedians.

This trait reached its nadir in the last of his three debates with then-Vice President Al Gore on October 17, 2000, at Washington University in St. Louis. The debate was conducted in the town hall format (the same format as the one in which George W. Bush's father had looked at his wristwatch and lost track of Marisa Hall's question). In this format, ordinary citizens had the opportunity to question the candidates directly. (There would be no follow-on questions for the son; he had learned from his father's mistake.) One young woman, Lisa Kee, asked:

> *How will your tax proposals affect me as a middle-class, 34-year old single person with no dependents?*

Governor George W. Bush replied:

> *You're going to get tax relief under my plan. You're not going to be targeted in or targeted out. Everybody who pays taxes is going to get tax relief. If you take care of an elderly in your home, you're going to get the personal exemption increased.*

"...take care of an elderly in your home"! His answer ignored the fact that the young woman had said that she has no dependents. Then, with hardly a pause for breath, he went on to say,

> *I think also what you need to think about is not the immediate, but what about Medicare?*

"Medicare"! Now his answer ignored the fact that she was 31 years away from eligibility for Medicare.

> *You get a plan that will include prescription drugs, a plan that will give you options. Now, I hope people understand that Medicare today is...is...is important, but it doesn't keep up with the new medicines. If you're a Medicare person, on Medicare, you don't get the new procedures. You're stuck in a time warp, in many ways. So it will be a modern Medicare system that trusts you to make a variety of options for you.*

His rambling answer continued to move further out on a limb.

> *You're going to live in a peaceful world. It'll be a world of peace, because we're going to have clearer...clear-sighted foreign policy based upon a strong military, and a mission that stands by our friends; a mission that doesn't try to be all things to all people. A judicious use of the military which well help keep the peace.*

He rambled farther and farther away from her question about his tax proposals.

> *You'll be in world, hopefully, that's more educated, so it's less likely you'll be harmed in your neighborhood. See, an educated child is one much more likely to be hopeful and optimistic. You'll be in a world in which fits into my philosophy; you know, the harder work...the harder you work the more you can keep. It's the American way. Government shouldn't be a heavy hand. That's what the federal government does to you. Should be a helping hand.*

Finally, as Governor Bush wound down his answer, he addressed the Roman Column in Lisa Kee's original question: his tax proposals.

And tax relief in the proposals I just described...

Then he offered a WIIFY to the 34-year old single person with no dependents.

...should be a good helping hand. [7.3]

"...should be a good helping hand." Spent by his ramble, Bush's WIIFY fizzled. He made it worse by speaking the words without any sense of conviction.

In his rush to Topspin with his own messages about Medicare, world peace, education, a strong military, his philosophy, and government policy, George W. Bush raced past Lisa Kee's question about his tax proposals with only a vague reference to them in his opening statement.

You're going to get tax relief under my plan. You're not going to be targeted in or targeted out. Everybody who pays taxes is going to get tax relief.

He was equally vague in his closing statement.

And tax relief in the proposals I just described should be a good helping hand.

With his rambling answer on seemingly unrelated subjects sandwiched between his first and last words, he appeared evasive. As a result, by the time he got to the end of his ramble, his Topspin fell flat in both delivery and substance.

A presenter or speaker must earn the right to Topspin by first answering the question.

The lesson here is that a presenter or speaker must earn the right to Topspin by *first* answering the question. Then, and only then, can you Topspin, and it will flow directly and appropriately from your answer.

The CEO of a startup company challenged by a potential investor concerned about the company's ability to compete against a larger, entrenched competitor could first answer by describing the company's competitive strategy and then conclude with Topspin, "We're confident that we can not only compete effectively, but will succeed in this market." Topspin to Point B. The Topspin then directly counters the challenge hurled in the question.

A salesperson challenged by a potential customer about the high price of a product could first answer by describing the total cost of ownership and then conclude with Topspin, "In the long run, you'll actually pay less." Topspin to a WIIFY.

A marketing manager challenged by the executive staff for seeking more advertising dollars in a time of cutbacks could first answer by reviewing the results of the previous ad campaign and then conclude with Topspin, "The ads will generate more revenues." Topspin to a WIIFY.

Topspin serves as the positive Yang to counter the negative Yin in the toughest question. If a question accuses you of being too expensive, too cheap, too small, too big, too late, too early, too light, too heavy, too narrow, too broad, too anything, you can counter the charge with your Topspin. Remember, however, that you must first neutralize the negative with your Buffer and then provide a substantial answer directly related to the Roman Column in the question, If you can, provide supporting evidence as well. After that, you are free to Topspin at will.

Despite his performance in the 2000 town-hall presidential debate, George W. Bush assumed the office for his first term. However, his advisors realized that he needed to appear more presidential in public, so they set about to make improvements. The result of their efforts became visible less than a year into office when he held a press conference at a high school in his home town, Crawford, Texas, on November 15, 2001.

In response to a question about U.S./Soviet relations, President Bush replied:

> *I believe the U.S./Russian relationship is one of them most important relationships that our country can have.*

This Roman Column in the question was the U.S./Soviet *relationship*, and so his answer immediately and directly related to the question, quid pro quo. Then, *after* his answer, he said:

> *And the stronger the relationship is...*

By restating the key word, "relationship," he linked forward to say,

> *...the more likely it is the world will be at peace.*

"The more likely it is the world will be at peace," a WIIFY for the world. Topspin. Then, restating the words, "the more likely," he linked forward again.

> *The more likely it is we'll be able to achieve a common objective, which is defeat the evil ones!*

"Common objective" is a synonym for Point B; Point B is a synonym for Topspin.

> *...that try to terrorize governments such as the United States and Russia. And we must defeat the evil ones...*

"We must defeat the evil ones," a restatement of his Point B and another Topspin. Because he was in a high school, he also gave the kids their very own WIIFY.

> *...in order for you all to grow up in a peaceful and prosperous world. [7.4]*

The quality improvement continued. After seasoning by the sobering events of 9/11, the economic downturn, and the war in Iraq, President Bush decided to run for a second term. On the day he officially filed to be a candidate, May 16, 2003, he held a brief press conference on the lawn at the White House (Figure 7.1).

FIGURE 7.1 *George W. Bush holds a press conference.*

In response to a question from a reporter about his prospects for reelection, President Bush said:

> *The American people will decide whether or not I deserve a second term.*

His quid pro quo answer related directly to the reporter's question and earned him the right to move on to his own message, his Topspin.

> *In the meantime, I am focusing my attention today on finding...helping people find work.*

"Helping people find work," a WIIFY for the electorate immediately after his answer...Topspin.

> *And that's where I'm going to be for a while. I want this economy to be robust and strong so that our fellow Americans who are looking for a job can find a job.*

Another WIIFY for the electorate...another Topspin.

We've also got a lot of work to do on the security front.

Here was still another Topspin, this time to reinforce his role as a wartime president, his Point B.

> *As John clearly pointed out, we've got an issue...we're dealing with countries from around the world to make sure that they know that the war on terror continues. No one should be complacent in the 21st century, the early stages of the 21st century, so long as al Qaeda moves. I've told the country that we've brought to justice about half of the al Qaeda network...operatives, key operatives. And so the other half still lives. And we'll find them, one at a time. [7.5]*

"We'll find them, one at a time," a restatement of his Point B, punctuated with determination in his voice and his expression.

In sum, President Bush delivered two strong Points B and two clear WIIFYs *after* his answer. Although the Points B and the WIIFYs were not *directly* in line with the Roman Column of his candidacy, the fact that he had provided an answer to the question released him to move on to his own messages, his Topspin.

By the time his run for reelection came around in 2004, George W. Bush had become even more accomplished at Topspin. Over the course of the campaign, he developed a reputation for staying on message relentlessly. At the same time, he also repeatedly attacked his opponent for "flip-flopping" his positions. John F. Kerry, to his own detriment, all too often obliged by shifting policy.

For most of the campaign, the senator's messaging either lacked focus or was inconsistent. In what was to become his *bete noire*, when a heckler at a campaign stop in West Virginia demanded to know why Kerry had voted *for* the invasion of Iraq and then voted *against* appropriating additional funds, he replied, "I actually did vote for the $87 billion before I voted against it." Bush pounced on the statement and derided it at every opportunity.

However, the president did not rely on negative attacks alone. They were far outweighed by many positive Topspins to his own agenda. This point is vividly apparent in the speeches he made during the homestretch of the campaign. A computer search of their texts on his website (http://www.whitehouse.gov/) finds that he repeated several key themes over and over, almost as a mantra.

- "Freedom is on the march"
- "A safer America, a stronger America"
- "We will prevail"
- "We have a moral responsibility"

The first three phrases related to the controversial war in Iraq. Despite the public opinion polls that showed widespread discontent with the operation and the almost daily horror stories from the region in the media, the president stuck to his guns and doggedly defended his choice. In his speeches, rallies, interviews, and press conferences, he stated and restated his conviction multiple times as Topspin.

The culminating instance of his effective use of Topspin occurred in the homestretch of the campaign, during the closing moments of his third and final debate against John F. Kerry, more of which you'll see in Chapter 9, "The Art of War." In response to the penultimate question of the debate, George W. Bush took the opportunity both to reaffirm his Point B and to disparage his rival.

> *My opponent keeps mentioning John McCain, and I'm glad he did. John McCain is for me for president because he understands I have the right view in winning the war on terror and that my plan will succeed in Iraq. And my opponent has got a plan of retreat and defeat in Iraq.*

"My plan will succeed in Iraq. And my opponent has got a plan of retreat and defeat in Iraq." In that one short statement, George W. Bush, in effect, succinctly summarized the entire 2004 election campaign: He was resolute in his convictions, while his opponent vacillated.

As important as was the issue of the war in Iraq, the fourth phrase in the preceding list, about moral responsibility, ultimately became even more important. Targeted at his core conservative support group, known as his "base," moral responsibility resonated with their all-important themes of patriotism, family, and religion, but more importantly, it also defined the president's positions on several other major controversial issues...same sex marriage, abortion, and stem cell research.

While the electorate as a whole was concerned with even more major issues...terrorism, taxes, jobs, health care, Social Security...in the end, moral responsibility was uppermost in their minds. According to Election Day exit polls, "When respondents were asked to pick the one issue that mattered most in choosing a president, "moral values" ranked first at 22%, surpassing the economy (20%), terrorism (19%), and Iraq (15%)." [7.6]

Even more telling was another Election Day exit poll of two of the most hotly contested swing states, which found that "about 8 out of 10 people in Florida and Ohio who voted for Mr. Bush said moral values had been a key factor in their decision." [7.7] Florida with its 27 electoral votes and Ohio with its 20 went to Bush, giving him a grand total of 286 electoral votes to Kerry's 252, with 270 needed to win. Topspin ruled.

Consistent to a fault, two months later, the president launched into his second term by delivering an Inaugural address in which he used the word "freedom" 27 times in the 20 minute speech.

In the discussion of the presidential debates in Chapter 9, you'll see more about how President Bush and Senator Kerry employed Topspin, as well as how they handled several other techniques that are so vital in the line of fire, but let's conclude this chapter with two other debates that provided classic examples of Topspin.

Lloyd Bentsen Topspins

In the U.S. presidential election of 1988 election in which George W. Bush's father, George H. Bush, ran against Michael Dukakis, their vice-presidential candidates, Dan Quayle, the senator from Indiana, and Lloyd Bentsen, the senator from Texas, also debated. The format for their single encounter was to respond to questions posed by a panel of journalists. When they assembled in the Omaha Civic Auditorium on October 5, 1988, Senator Quayle was struggling with the stigma of his youth and inexperience, and the journalists, true to their nature, went after his weak spot.

First, Judy Woodruff of the Public Broadcasting Service challenged Quayle's maturity. Then, Brit Hume of ABC NEWS took up the cudgel, challenging him twice more on the same subject and, when his turn came, so did Tom Brokaw of NBC NEWS.

> *Senator Quayle, I don't mean to beat this drum until it has no more sound in it. But to follow up on Brit Hume's question, when you said that it was a hypothetical situation, it is, sir, after all, the reason that we're here tonight, because you are running not just for Vice President...*

The audience in the auditorium, sensing the intensity of the panelists' pursuit of this vital issue, broke into applause. Then, Brokaw continued.

> *...And if you cite the experience that you had in Congress, surely you must have some plan in mind about what you would do if it fell to you to become President of the United States, as it has to so many Vice Presidents just in the last 25 years or so.*

With a touch of exasperation, Quayle replied to Brokaw's challenge:

> *Let me try to answer the question one more time. I think this is the fourth time that I've had this question.*

Brokaw interjected, holding up three fingers.

> *The third time.*

Brokaw was wrong. It *was* the fourth time, but in his frustration, Quayle accepted the correction.

> *Three times that I've had this question...and I will try to answer it again for you, as clearly as I can, because the question you are asking is what kind of qualifications does Dan Quayle have to be president...*

Brokaw shook his head from side to side. That was *not* the question he was asking. Quayle saw Brokaw's negative reaction and tried to reframe his question.

> *...what kind of qualifications do I have...*

But Brokaw continued to shake his head. As if to emphasize his dissatisfaction, he also sat back and folded his arms across his chest. You'll recall from Chapter 5, "Retake the Floor," that the audience's physical reaction to whether the presenter has heard the question or not is completely involuntary for all human beings...even professional journalists like Tom Brokaw.

Suddenly, Quayle realized that the Roman Column was his *plan* and not his *qualifications*. His eyes widened and his voice rose in confidence to state it.

> *...and what would I do in this kind of a situation.*

Quayle finally got it right and Brokaw nodded in assent. Quayle went on for a minute to outline what he would do, and then concluded his answer with Topspin to his qualifications.

> *It is not just age; it's accomplishments, it's experience. I have far more experience than many others that sought*

the office of vice president of this country. I have as much experience in the Congress as Jack Kennedy did when he sought the presidency. I will be prepared to deal with the people in the Bush administration, if that unfortunate event would ever occur.

During Quayle's answer, the television image cut from a close up of Quayle to a wide shot that included Lloyd Bentsen, his eyebrows raised in incredulity (Figure 7.2).

▲ **FIGURE 7.2** *Senator Lloyd Bentsen reacts to Dan Quayle.*

At that point, Judy Woodruff turned the floor over to Senator Bentsen for his rebuttal. Senator Bentsen *began* his answer with Topspin.

Senator, I served with Jack Kennedy, I knew Jack Kennedy, Jack Kennedy was a friend of mine. Senator, you are no Jack Kennedy. [7.8]

As powerful and as famous was Lloyd Bentsen's Topspin, there was another more powerful and more famous.

Ronald Reagan Topspins

On October 28, 1984, incumbent President Ronald Reagan met Senator Walter Mondale of Minnesota at the Municipal Auditorium in Kansas City in a presidential debate with a format similar to the Quayle-Bentsen match: responding to the questions from a panel of journalists. During the debate, Henry Trewhitt, the diplomatic correspondent for *The Baltimore Sun*, asked President Reagan:

> *You already are the oldest president in history and some of your staff say you were tired after your most recent encounter with Mr. Mondale. I recall yet that President Kennedy had to go days on end very little sleep during the Cuba missile crisis. Is there any doubt in your mind that you would be able to function in such circumstances?*

Ronald Reagan, known as the Great Communicator, and deservedly so, replied promptly with a crisp three-word answer,

> *Not at all.*

Then, he then immediately switched to the offensive with an agile Topspin for the ages.

> *And, Mr. Trewhitt, I want you to know also I will not make age an issue of this campaign. I am not going to exploit for political purposes my opponent's youth and inexperience. [7.9]*

Even his opponent, Senator Mondale, knew he was in the presence of a master of the game, and he laughed along with the peals of laughter from the audience (Figure 7.3).

▲ **FIGURE 7.3** *Ronald Reagan Topspins Walter Mondale.*

Ronald Reagan's Topspin and Colin Powell's Key Word Buffers are examples of virtuosos at their best. Neither skill comes easily; each of them is counterintuitive to the natural tendency of results-driven presenters to jump directly to answers and then to keep moving. Each of these skills requires an effort to learn. That takes *discipline*, the next of the core martial arts skills, and the subject of the next chapter.

CHAPTER 8

Preparation

(Martial Art: Discipline)

The most important part begins even before you put your hand on the sword.

Jyoseishi Kendan
By Matsura Seizan (8.1)
(1760–1841)

In the martial arts, the discipline required to learn new skills carries virtually the same weight as the skills themselves. Every martial arts treatise sets forth both the underlying philosophy and the rigorous steps required to attain mastery. In karate, the learning progression is marked by the graduated color coding of the uniform belts. Starting with the beginners' white belt, the levels of achievement for most schools ascend through yellow, orange, green, blue, and brown, culminating in the coveted black belt. It takes years of disciplined practice and preparation to ascend through all the levels. Only the best can achieve the highest level. Although learning to answer tough questions might not be as daunting as a lethal sport, you would do well to apply Thomas Edison's formula for genius, 1% inspiration and 99% perspiration, by working very hard before you put *your* hand on the sword.

Ever since the U.S. presidential election of 1960, when the underdog, John F. Kennedy, was able to reverse the field against the favorite, Richard M. Nixon, in the first-ever televised debate, such matches have played a key role in every political campaign. Although the turnabout was largely attributed to Kennedy's superior presentation skills, preparation also played a significant role.

Don Hewitt, the driving force behind CBS' *60 Minutes*, happened to have been the television director of that historic debate and, in his autobiography, he described some of the preparations. Kennedy arrived in Chicago three days before the debate to prepare and even took some time in the late September sun to get tanned. Nixon, in spite of the fact that he was fighting an infection, spent his time campaigning vigorously right up to the day of debate. He arrived at the television studio exhausted and underweight, his ill-fitting clothing hanging loosely. Nixon's aides hurriedly applied a slapdash coat of a product called "Lazy Shave" to his characteristically heavy beard and made him look pasty. Kennedy used a light coat of makeup. In the hot lights of the studio, Nixon perspired through his "Lazy Shave," which gave him a worse appearance than a five o'clock shadow. [8.2]

Kennedy's aides had surveyed the studio in advance and advised him to wear a dark suit to contrast with the light blue backdrop of the set. In black-and-white television, the light blue translated to grey. Nixon wore a light suit that translated into the same monochrome value as the background and made him look washed out (Figure 8.1).

▲ **FIGURE 8.1** *John F. Kennedy and Richard M. Nixon debate.*

Nixon had held a slim lead in the public opinion polls right up to the day of the debate. The day after the debate, Sindlinger and Company, a Philadelphia research organization, conducted a telephone poll. Those poll respondents who had watched on television thought Kennedy won, while those who had listened on the radio thought Nixon won. [8.3] This gave Kennedy a lead that he held until his victory in November.

From that moment on, media consultants became as important as positioning strategists in political campaigns and, from that moment on, preparation became an absolute imperative for debates. Although there were no other presidential debates until 1976 when President Gerald R. Ford met Georgia Governor Jimmy Carter, they became set pieces thereafter every four years.

In each of those years, each candidate, accompanied by key staff members, decamped to sequestered retreats. There, with the thoroughness of the allies planning for D-Day, each candidate ramped up to the debate with intensive preparation. Ford and Carter prepared diligently, and so did their successors [8.4]:

- 1980: Ronald Reagan, Jimmy Carter, and John Anderson
- 1984: Ronald Reagan and Walter Mondale
- 1988: George H. Bush and Michael Dukakis
- 1992: George H. Bush, Bill Clinton, and Ross Perot
- 1996: Bill Clinton and Bob Dole
- 2000: Al Gore and George W. Bush
- 2004: George W. Bush and John F. Kerry

Over a period of weeks the candidates reviewed research, brainstormed, refined positions, viewed opponent's tapes, and held mock debates with carefully chosen stand-ins. They even had rehearsal studios built to replicate those of the actual venue. Over the years, each debate provided lessons for subsequent debates. Cumulatively, the candidates and their campaign staffs compiled a long list of what to do and, more important, what not to do.

By the time President George W. Bush was to debate Massachusetts Senator John F. Kerry in the 2004 election, presidential debates had evolved into a sophisticated science. The Bush team set up shop at the president's ranch in Crawford, Texas, while the Kerry team gathered at a resort 40 miles outside of Madison, Wisconsin. You'll see a detailed analysis of the results of their efforts in the next chapter, but let's first look at how preparation impacted another debate with which you are already familiar.

It's another and deeper look at the NAFTA debate between Vice President Al Gore and Ross Perot on the *Larry King Live* television program. In Chapter 1, "The Critical Dynamics of Q&A," you saw how Perot flared up at Gore in response to a challenge, but that was only one of many such outbursts during the 90-minute broadcast. Each of them was provoked by the deliberate strategy the Gore team had developed in anticipation of the debate. Their preparatory efforts were described in an article in *The Atlantic Monthly* by James Fallows.

> *Gore, meanwhile, spent the two weeks before the debate studying Perot's bearing and his character, while relying on his staff to dig up the goods on Perot's past...[they] prepared an omnibus edition of Perot's speeches, statements, and interviews about NAFTA, and also tapes of Perot in action. Gore studied them on his own and then assembled a team at the Naval Observatory...the vice president's official residence*

One of the key members of that team was Greg Simon, Gore's domestic policy advisor. Simon told Fallows about the key strategy that emerged from those sessions:

> *If you've dealing with a hothead, you make him mad...You've got a crazy man, you make him show it...He'll be fine as long as everybody sits there and listens to him, but if you start interrupting him, he'll lose it. [8.5]*

Gore proceeded to interrupt Perot repeatedly. In fact, Perot complained to Larry King, to Al Gore, and to the television audience about the interruptions *eight* times during the first half of the program. By midway through, Perot was steaming mad and operating on a short fuse. Nonetheless, he pressed ahead with his cause by turning to the camera and addressing the television audience with yet another blast against NAFTA in general, and Mexico in particular.

> *All right folks, the Rio Grande River is the most polluted river in the Western Hemisphere...*

Right on cue, Gore interrupted.

> *Wait a minute. Can I respond to this first?*

Larry King tried to intervene.

> *Yeah, let him respond.*

By now, Perot was in no way going to let Gore respond.

> *The Tijuana River is the most...they've had to close it...*

Larry King asked,

> *But all of this is without NAFTA, right?*

Gore persisted.

> *Yeah, and let me respond to this, if I could, would you...*

Perot ignored Gore and turned to address Larry King.

> *Larry, Larry, this is after years of U.S. companies going to Mexico, living free...*

Larry King tried to clarify:

> *But they could do that without NAFTA.*

Perot spoke past Gore, directly to Larry King:

> *But we can stop that without NAFTA and we can stop that with a good NAFTA.*

Gore, sitting at Perot's side, asked:

> *How do you stop that without NAFTA?*

Peeved, Perot swung around to face Gore and replied testily:

> *Just make...just cut that out. Pass a few simple laws on this, make it very, very clear...*

Quite innocently, Gore asked:

> *Pass a few simple laws on Mexico?*

His anger rising again, Perot, shook his head, then dropped it like a bull about to charge, and said:

No.

Gore persisted, quietly, but firmly.

How do you stop it without NAFTA?

Icily, Perot replied:

Give me your whole mind.

"Give me your whole mind." Perot addressed the vice president of the United States as if he was an errant employee! The vice president of the United States smiled back broadly, and said:

Yeah, I'm listening. I haven't heard the answer, but go ahead.

Chiding back, Perot snapped:

That's because you haven't quit talking.

Gore replied:

Well, I'm listening...

And then for the third time, Gore calmly repeated his question.

How do you stop it without NAFTA?

Perot would not be calmed.

OK, are you going to listen? Work on it! [8.6]

"Work on it!" More disdain and more petulance from Perot. The sum total of all his contentious behavior came a cropper the next day in the public opinion polls: The undecided respondents dramatically swung in favor of NAFTA (please refer to Figure 1.1).

Lessons Learned

The key takeaway from this chapter is its main theme: discipline. By all accounts, Al Gore focused his efforts on what he did *before he put his hand on the sword*. Perot was notoriously delinquent in preparation. Having campaigned against NAFTA for three months before the debate, Perot "cruised toward the discussion as if it would be another episode of the Ross-and-Larry mutual-admiration show," according to Fallows. [8.7]

During Perot's run for the presidency the year before the NAFTA debate, he had retained Ed Rollins, one of the most respected political consultants in the game. Six weeks later, Rollins resigned in dismay at Perot's refusal to take his advice. The advice for you is to take Gore's offsite encampment activity as a positive role model to develop two important techniques:

- **Prepare**. Anticipate the worst-case scenario. Make a list of the questions you do not want to hear. Find the Roman Columns in the tough questions as well as the non-challenging ones. Develop your positions on every major issue, especially the negative ones. Gather your supporting evidence. Do your research. Define your overall strategy as Al Gore did. Do all of this well in advance of your mission-critical Q&A session!
- **Verbalize**. This is the technique you first read about in Chapter 5, "Retake the Floor." Speak your words aloud in practice just as you will during your actual Q&A session. Verbalization is the equivalent of spring training in baseball, previews of Broadway shows and, most pertinent, the mock rehearsals that precede political debates. The latter examples have even more specificity and urgency for you. Politicians speak far more often than do mere mortals, and even more so during their campaigns. By the time they get down the homestretch to the debates, they have spoken their messages countless times.

You do not have that advantage. Organize practice sessions to prepare for your actual Q&A session. Enlist your colleagues to fire tough questions at you. Verbalize your Buffers. Verbalize your answers until they are succinct and to the point. Verbalize your Topspin to every answer. Verbalize repeatedly, like a tennis volley.

This is a technique I recommend to all my private clients, and particularly to companies preparing their IPO road shows, the most mission-critical of all business presentations. I urge CEOs and CFOs to volley their responses to their list of tough questions over and over until their returns of serves snap like whips. I urge you to treat every Q&A session as your IPO road show. Snap your whip.

CHAPTER

9

The Art of War

(Martial Art: Self-Control)

Those who win every battle are not really skillful...those who render others' armies helpless without fighting are the best of all.

General Sun Tzu
The Art of War [9.1]

The martial arts are called "arts" and not "sciences" because success or failure depends more on artful application than on any formula or equation. The central application of these arts is to the battle itself. It is with good reason that General Sun Tzu's 2,500 year-old book is found on the shelves of many modern businesses today. Here in the twenty-first century, its ideas have become a treatise for combat in business, if not a primer for *any* conflict in life. But the good General did not originate the idea of winning without fighting. The concept goes all the way back to the Old Testament, "*He that is slow to anger is better than the mighty*" (Proverbs 16:32).

Fighting is synonymous with the contentious, evasive, and defensive behavior that you saw exhibited respectively by Ross Perot, Trent Lott, and Bob Newhart. Each of them demonstrated negative behavior that produced negative perceptions in their audiences, and none of them won his battle.

Contentiousness is the most damaging of these behaviors because it represents loss of control, the opposite of the desired objective of *Effective Management.* To achieve this positive subliminal perception, you must *never* react to tough questions with anger; instead *always* respond with firm, but calm resolve...which brings us full circle back to the Introduction where we set out with a one-word summary of *all* the techniques in this book: *control.*

Never react to tough questions with anger; instead *always* respond with firm, but calm resolve.

Al Gore won his battle with Ross Perot *without fighting*. His interruptions caused Perot to lose control and become belligerent. Gore then *rendered his opponent helpless* by smiling...by using *agility to counter force.*

The Art of Agility

Agility requires artistry to succeed. Too strong a touch can overshoot the mark; too light can fall short. Martial art masters, athletes, and dancers, all of whom quest for physical agility, understand this all too well. They experience performances of sheer perfection and others of abject failure. The same can be true of verbal agility in the line of fire of tough questions.

Al Gore is a case study in point that ranges from his campaign and election in 1992, through his campaign and reelection in 1996, and all the way to his own run for the presidency in 2000. The progression of his performances in his mission-critical debates provides an object lesson that all the experience, all the knowledge, all the disciplined preparation and all the science in the world will be for naught without the artful application of agility, without self-control.

Force: 1992

A year before his masterful triumph over Ross Perot in the NAFTA debate, Al Gore used force against force instead of agility. In his first run for national office, Gore met Dan Quayle in a vice presidential debate on October 13, 1992, in Atlanta, Georgia. Quayle, who had been burnt four years earlier by the memorable Topspin of Lloyd Bentsen you saw in Chapter 7, "Topspin in Action," was determined to not to allow history to repeat itself.

Quayle and his team decided to reverse the classic football maxim, *the best offense is a good defense*, by vigorously taking the offensive to Gore. Quayle prepared for the contest in extensive practice sessions with a formidable stand-in for Gore, then-New

Hampshire Senator Warren Rudman, an aggressive gadfly whose subsequent autobiography was appropriately titled, *Combat.* Practice *with* Rudman made Quayle highly combative.

About a third of the way into the debate, Gore spoke of a talk he had had with some citizens who had lost their jobs. Then, he turned toward Quayle and asked:

> *Do you seriously believe that we ought to continue the same policies that have created the worst economy since the Great Depression?*

Rather than answer Gore's question, Quayle launched into an attack.

> *I hope that when you talked to those people you said: "And the first thing that Bill Clinton and I are going to do is to raise $150 billion in new taxes."*

Gore objected.

> *You got that wrong, too!*

Ignoring the challenge, Quayle continued his attack.

> *And the first...that is part of your plan.*

Gore objected again, shaking his head.

> *No, it's not!*

Raising his voice, Quayle repeated his charge, wagging his finger at Gore (Figure 9.1).

> *A hundred and fifty billion dollars in new taxes.*

▲ **FIGURE 9.1** *Dan Quayle wags his finger at Al Gore.*

Quayle threw out his arms and shrugged his shoulders.

> *Well, you're going to disavow your plan.*

Gore tried to explain.

> *Listen, what we're proposing...*

Quayle stepped up the intensity.

> *You know what you're doing, you know what you're doing? You're pulling a Clinton.*

Several people in the audience hooted with laughter, as Quayle explained his terminology.

> *And you know what a Clinton is? And you know what Clinton is? A Clinton is, is what he says...he says one thing one day and another thing the next day...you try to have both sides of the issues. The fact of the matter is that you are proposing $150 billion in new taxes.*

Shaking his head again, Gore objected to Quayle's third statement of his charge.

No!

Quayle continued his assault.

And I hope that you talk to the people in Tennessee...

Gore fought back vainly.

No, we're not!

Undeterred, Quayle pressed forward, speaking to Gore as if he was a schoolchild.

...and told them that...

Smiling wanly, Gore protested.

You can say it all you want but it doesn't make it true.

On a roll, Quayle unleashed a crescendo of further accusations.

> *...[they were] going to have new taxes. I hope you talked to them about the fact that you were going to increase spending to $220 billion. I'm sure what you didn't talk to them about...*

Now Quayle turned away from Gore and looked straight into the camera to address the national television audience.

> *...was about how we're going to reform the health care system, like the president wants to do.*

Quayle culminated his tirade against Gore and Clinton with a strong Topspin to his own Point B.

> *He wants to go out and to reform the health care system...*

For good measure, Quayle added one more layer of Topspin, to a WIIFY for the electorate.

> *...so that every American will have available to them affordable health insurance. [9.2]*

Although Quayle won the exchange, he did not win the war. He could not slow the two powerful forces of George H. Bush's inability to address the nation's economic difficulties and Bill Clinton's charisma that swept the Clinton-Gore team into the White House.

However, Gore could have done better in the debate. He could have employed the agility he would bring into play against Perot a year later. Instead, Gore met Quayle's force with force by shouting back at his accuser's charges, "You got that wrong!," "No!," "No, it's not!," and "It doesn't make it true."

Imagine if instead, when Quayle accused the Clinton-Gore ticket of planning to raise $150 billion in new taxes, Gore had neutralized Quayle's charge with a Buffer of the Roman Column of their tax plan by saying,

> *Let's compare our tax plan to yours.*

Then, with the playing field leveled, imagine if Gore had answered,

> *Remember Dan, it was George Bush who said, "Read my lips... no new taxes," and then raised them.*

At that point, Gore could have even gone on to add Topspin with *both* a Point B and a WIIFY by concluding with,

> *The Clinton-Gore tax plan provides incentives for investment in job-creating activities...to get our economy going again.*

In the end, however, it was the electorate, rather than Al Gore, that provided the ultimate Topspin.

Agility: 1996

Just as Quayle was able to reverse field, so did Al Gore when he and Bill Clinton campaigned for reelection four years later. Their opponents were two formidable politicians: Bob Dole, the veteran senate majority leader, was the Republican presidential candidate and Jack Kemp, the vice presidential candidate. Gore was to engage in a one-on-one debate with Kemp on October 9, 1996, in St. Petersburg, Florida.

Kemp would be a much more formidable opponent than the callow Quayle or the cantankerous Perot. Kemp had served nine terms in the House of Representatives and four years as Secretary of Housing and Urban Development, but his greatest claim to fame was as a professional football quarterback. He had played with the San Diego Chargers and the Buffalo Bills and led the latter to two American Football League championships. In all his public appearances, Kemp played the football hero image to the hilt, sporting an enormous, jewel-bedecked championship ring on his right hand for all the world to see. Moreover, he had developed a public persona as a charming, garrulous speaker.

Although Gore's victory over Perot three years earlier had earned him new respect as a debater, he still carried the stigma, repeated ad infinitum by the late-night television comedians, of a stiff public speaker.

Once again, Gore and his team treated the debate as a major challenge and assembled at an offsite in Florida they called a "debate camp." One of the strategies to emerge from their sessions was to level the playing field with Kemp by defusing the preconceived images of the football hero versus the wooden statue.

In his opening statement of the debate, Gore said,

> *I'd like to start by offering you a deal, Jack. If you won't use any football stories...*

Kemp took the bait. Seen in a television split screen, Kemp chuckled at the remark and then obliged even further by lifting his hand to pantomime throwing a football. His championship ring sparkled as he did. Meanwhile Gore struck an exaggerated deadpan expression (Figure 9.2).

▲ **FIGURE 9.2** *Jack Kemp and Al Gore debate.*

Then, Gore concluded his offer.

> *...I won't tell any of my warm and humorous stories about chlorofluorocarbon abatement.*

The self-deprecating humor produced not only a laugh from the audience, but agreement and capitulation from Kemp.

> *It's a deal.*

As the audience laughed louder, Gore broke into a big grin, and Kemp capitulated again.

> *I can't even pronounce it. [9.3]*

After this running head start, Gore went on to combat Kemp on both style and substance. Kemp, known for his verbosity, had three instances in which he lost track of the time, while Gore's well-rehearsed answers were crisp and succinct.

Immediately after the end of the debate, CNN/*USA Today*/Gallup conducted a poll with a focus group of registered voters who had watched the debate. The first question they were asked was, "Regardless of which candidate you happen to support, who do you think did the better job in the debate, Al Gore or Jack Kemp?" The results: Gore 57%, Kemp: 28%. [9.4]

Once again, the Gore debate strategy, preparation, and execution, paid off. His double advantage over Kemp in the poll, combined with Clinton's charismatic advantage over Dole, gave the incumbents the momentum to sweep to victory on Election Day. The die was cast. With his decisive conquests of Jack Kemp and, a year later, Ross Perot, Gore was now a debater to be reckoned with and, as a virtual incumbent, the Democratic candidate for president in the next election.

Agility and Force: 2000

In 2000, Gore's opponent was then Texas Governor George W. Bush, a candidate saddled with the image of a man challenged by the English language. Despite Gore's successes in the debate arena and his two terms in office, he could not shake the wooden label. The media and the late-night comics had a field day lampooning both candidates.

Notwithstanding the satire, Gore had the edge. By every estimate, he was expected to dominate the debates. In fact, the issue of *The Atlantic Monthly* that contained the James Fallows article in the previous chapter had on its cover a caricature of Gore baring feral fangs.

In their first debate, at the University of Massachusetts in Boston, Massachusetts, on October 3, 2000, Al Gore forsook the agility that had served him so well in the past and came out roaring like a lion. Fueled by his disciplined preparation (and very likely, a strong dose of overconfidence), Gore applied all his rhetorical strengths and accumulated knowledge against George W. Bush. Gore's statements and rebuttals were filled with aggressive and divisive words like "wrong," "not," "differences," "mistake," and "opposite." [9.5]

His manner was also combative, continually punctuated by condescending sighs, derisive head-shaking, scornful frowns, and disdainful eye-rolling (Figure 9.3).

▲ **FIGURE 9.3** *Al Gore sighs at George W. Bush.*

This arrogant behavior immediately boomeranged. The television broadcasters had a camera isolated on Gore for reaction shots. Their news directors took the output of this camera and edited all his disdainful expressions into a rapid-cut sequence. They ran the montage repeatedly in their local and national broadcasts.*

*You can see our version of this montage on the companion DVD, available at www.powerltd.com.

Public and professional criticism rained down on the vice president, implicating not only his haughty attitude, but the accuracy of his statements.

In response, Gore made a sharp about face and came out like a lamb in the second debate held on October 11, 2000, at Wake Forest University in Winston-Salem, North Carolina. During the 90 minutes, Gore expressed agreement with his opponent *seven* times on major issues, undershooting his intended mark by a country mile. Humbly, at the end of the broadcast, Gore even offered an apology for his exaggerations in the earlier debate:

> *I got some of the details wrong last week in some of the examples that I used, Jim, and I'm sorry about that. [9.6]*

The most telling reaction to Gore's docile performance came from a CNN analyst:

> *Whatever happened to Al the Barbarian? The man who knows better than anybody how to destroy an opponent with his mastery of the facts? Where was the clever repartee? Why did he let George Bush get away with so much without going in for the kill? Al Gore was emasculated by his handlers. He sat there as if he were embarrassed to be on the same stage and ashamed of taking up so much time. He let pass countless openings to unmask Bush as uninformed. He was so damned nice, he ended up drowning in his own honey. [9.7]*

In reaction to reams of criticism like this, Gore reversed field again and swung back to his aggressive ways. In the third debate on October 17, 2000, at Washington University in St. Louis, Missouri, Gore went on the offensive. Remember that this is the very same town-hall format debate you read about in Chapter 7 when George W. Bush, left to his own devices in an answer to Lisa Kee, wandered off track and fizzled. In the following section, which occurred *earlier* in the debate, you'll see Gore's most pronounced attack and, more important, how Bush handled it.

The moderator, Jim Lehrer of the *PBS News Hour* asked:

> *Would you agree that you two agree on a national patient's bill of rights?*

A revved-up Al Gore replied emphatically, "Absolutely not," and then went on to discuss a proposal pending in Congress called The Dingle-Norwood Bill, which would provide legislation on HMOs. Gore then went on to say:

> *And I specifically would like to know whether Governor Bush will support the Dingle-Norwood bill, which is the main one pending.*

Lehrer said:

> *Governor Bush, you may answer that if you'd like. But also I'd like to know how you see the differences between the two of you, and we need to move on.*

The Governor rose from his seat and began to address his answer to the town-hall audience.

> *Well, the difference is that I can get it done. That I can get something positive done on behalf of the people. That's what the question in this campaign is about...*

As Bush continued his answer, Gore stood up, and started to walk across the stage, directly toward his opponent, almost menacingly. Unaware of Gore's move, Bush continued:

> *...It's not only what's your philosophy and what's your position on issues, but can you get things done?*

In the middle of his statement, Bush turned to see Gore approaching (Figure 9.4).

▲ **FIGURE 9.4** *Al Gore approaches George W. Bush.*

Bush paused for a beat, then nodded at Gore and smiled, evoking titters from the audience. Then, Bush turned back to the audience and said:

> *And I believe I can.*

The audience titters gave way to laughter. Gore stopped in front of Bush and forced a broad smile that stood in sharp contrast to his rigid body language and insisted:

> *What about the Dingle-Norwood bill?*

Lehrer interceded.

> *All right. We're going to go now to another...*

Bush said:

> *I'm not quite through. Let me finish.*

Lehrer acceded.

> *All right. Go...*

Bush went on:

> *I talked about the principles and the issues that I think are important in a patients' bill of rights. It's kind of [a] Washington, D.C. focus. Well, it's in this committee or it's got this sponsor. If I'm the president, we're going to have emergency room care, we'll have gag orders, we'll have direct access to OB/GYN. People will be able to take their HMO insurance company to court. That's what I've done in Texas and that's the kind of leadership style I'll bring to Washington. [9.8]*

George W. Bush did to Al Gore what Al Gore had done to Ross Perot: He countered hostility with agility and neutralized his opponent. To add insult to Gore's injury, Bush, with a virtual free pass from the moderator, concluded his exchange with strong Topspin; an advantage he neglected to take *later* in that same debate in his exchange with Lisa Kee.

A *The Wall Street Journal*/NBC News poll about the effects of the debate on public opinion gave George W. Bush a seven point advantage over Al Gore. [9.9]

How did this upset occur? How was the underdog able to give the favorite a run for his money? The answer lies in a dynamic that often occurs in a contest of mismatched opponents: *lower expectations*. All the underdog has to do is show up and not foul up. All George W. Bush had to do was avoid mistakes; anything less than a total thrashing by Gore would be a success for Bush. In fact, the Bush team, intentionally or not, presaged its debate strategy by naming its 2000 campaign jet airplane, "Great Expectations."

The debates were Al Gore's to lose and, given his previous successes and his own great expectations...he did. Of course, George W. Bush did become the president in an election so tight the Supreme Court had to decide the disputed vote in the swing state of Florida, but imagine if Al Gore had dominated the debates as he was expected to?

In the first debate, Gore abandoned agility and became the assailant. In the second, he over-compensated the opposite way into passivity. By the third, in trying to reassert his power, he overshot his mark, lost his touch…and control.

Gore beat his two previous opponents with the *agility* of a judo master. He made Ross Perot the assailant by provoking his volatile temperament with interruptions, and he threw Jack Kemp off balance by puncturing his jock charm with self-deprecating humor. When Gore made his *forceful* "in-your-face" move on George W. Bush, Gore became the attacker. When Bush smiled at Gore's menacing approach, he turned Gore's own former weapon against him; the weapon you would do well to learn…**agility counters force**.

You would do well to learn: agility counters force.

Agility and Force: 2004

By the time President George W. Bush and Senator John F. Kerry met for the first of their three scheduled debates, each of them had staked out a reputation as a formidable debater. The president by virtue of his victory over Al Gore four years earlier; and the senator, a champion debater since his student days at St. Paul's prep school and Yale University, had honed his skills on floor of the U.S. Senate for 20 years. The two men were, by most rhetorical standards, considered equals.

Moreover, the grueling political campaign of that summer…one of the most polarized in the history of presidential elections…had etched their diametrically divergent platforms indelibly. Both of them had sharpened their positions on key issues and had delivered them many times over. Both of them were also highly skilled at Topspin: repeatedly making calls to action by asking for the vote, their Point B, and repeatedly pointing out how that vote would bring security, tax relief, health care, and the like, to the electorate, their WIIFYs. However, there were several other factors in play in their debates, having to do with agility and force.

After nearly half a century, the accumulated intelligence about televised political debates had grown to a canon of enormous proportions. The respective Bush and Kerry committees, determined to learn from history and avoid mistakes, negotiated for months to establish a set of intricate guidelines. They finally came to terms in a Memorandum of Understanding that ran 32 pages and covered everything from the sublime, the rules of engagement, to the ridiculous, their notepaper, pens, and pencils.

Echoes of history reverberated behind every stipulation: control of the studio temperature to avoid a repeat of the perspiration that betrayed Richard Nixon; control of the town-hall audience microphones to avoid a follow-on question like that of Marisa Hall; a system of warning lights (green at 30 seconds, yellow at 15 seconds, red at 5 and flashing red to stop) installed on each lectern to avoid the difficulties Jack Kemp had with time; and a ban on television-camera reaction shots to avoid images of a candidate looking at his wristwatch as did George H. Bush or showing disdain for his opponent's remarks as did Al Gore. Every aspect of the debates was covered in excruciating detail, right down to the exact positions and heights (50 inches) of the podiums.

This latter specification was to boomerang against George W. Bush in the first debate on September 30, 2004, at the University of Miami in Coral Gables, Florida. The podiums were to be of equal heights, but the candidates were not. John Kerry is 6'4", and George W. Bush is 5'11", which caused the incumbent to hunch over his lectern, while the tall senator stood erect and free of his. The presenter behavior/audience perception dynamic reared its forceful head and struck George W. Bush between the shoulder blades: The President looked challenged, and the challenger looked presidential (Figure 9.5).

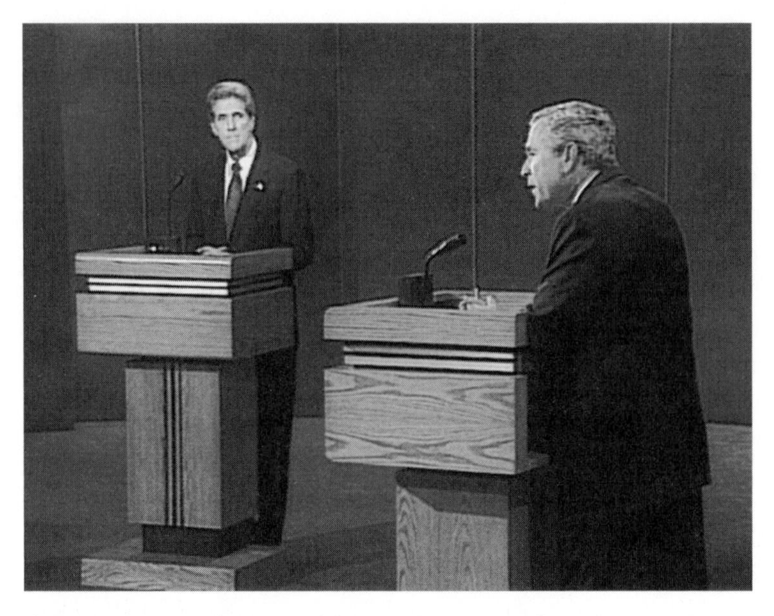

▲ **FIGURE 9.5** *John Kerry debates George W. Bush.*

The timing system also worked against the incumbent and for the challenger. With the warning lights in constant view of the 62.5 million people in the television audience, the president, on several occasions, ran out of things to say while the yellow light was on, leaving 15 precious seconds unused, during which he might have added a supporting point. Worse still, when he stopped speaking, his voice hung in midair, making him appear uncertain.

The most glaring of these instances came late in the debate, in his response to a question about his relationship with Vladimir Putin, the Russian president. The American president started his answer briskly, but half way through, he began to slow down and to punctuate his words with long pauses and repeated "Uhs."

> *I've got a good relation with Vladimir. And it's important that we do have a good relation, because that enables me to better...uh...comment to him, and to better to discuss with him, some of the decisions he makes.*

I found that, in this world, that...uh...that it's important to establish good personal relationships with people so that when you have disagreements, you're able to disagree in a way that...uh...is effective. And so I've told him my opinion.

I look forward to discussing it more with him, as time goes on...uh...Russia is a country in transition... uh...Vladimir is...uh...going to have to make some hard choices. And I think it's very important for the American president, as well as other Western leaders, to remind him of the great benefits of democracy, that democracy... uh...will best...uh...help the people realize their hopes and aspirations and dreams. And...uh...I will continue working with him over the next four years.

When the president concluded, the yellow light was still lit.

Conversely, the senator, who had developed a reputation as being long-winded, was able to control the length of his statements with the timing lights, a skill he had sharpened in four full 90-minute practice sessions just prior to the debate. As part of his practice, he also learned to punctuate his statements by finishing them succinctly, often with Topspin, just as the red light lit.

John Kerry also used Topspin to punctuate...and puncture...one of his opponent's primary rhetorical themes. Throughout the campaign, Bush had disparaged Kerry's record of shifting policies and repeatedly labeled them "flip-flopping." In that first debate, the president hammered home this theme at least eight times, accusing the senator of "changing positions," "inconsistency," "mixed signals," or "mixed messages," culminating in one *forceful* fusillade:

You cannot lead if you send mixed messages. Mixed messages send the wrong signals to our troops. Mixed messages send the wrong signals to our allies. Mixed messages send the wrong signals to the Iraqi citizens.

One of John Kerry's primary slogans, repeated many times over on the campaign trail, was that the "W" in George W. Bush's name "stands for wrong. Wrong choices, wrong direction for America." When the senator's turn came to reply to his opponent's fusillade, he countered it with a swift burst of Topspin:

It's one thing to be certain, but you can be certain and be wrong.

At another point in the debate, Kerry used Topspin again to counteract the flip-flopping label. He did it during an exchange that began when the president seized the opportunity to once again remind the 62.5 million viewers about the senator's *bete noir* that you read about in Chapter 7.

He voted against the $87-billion supplemental to provide equipment for our troops, and then said he actually did vote for it before he voted against it. Not what a commander in chief does when you're trying to lead troops.

The moderator, Jim Lehrer, gave the floor back to John Kerry,

Senator Kerry, 30 seconds.

Kerry began his rebuttal by taking responsibility.

Well, you know, when I talked about the $87 billion, I made a mistake in how I talk about the war...

Then he concluded with Topspin,

...But the president made a mistake in invading Iraq. Which is worse?

The Topspin worked: The statement was played and replayed as a sound bite on the television news programs. Unfortunately, in another exchange just a few moments later, the senator reverted to form when Jim Lehrer asked him:

Are Americans now dying in Iraq for a mistake?

Mr. Kerry replied,

> *No.*

By contradicting himself, in effect, he admitted to his tragic flaw, and shot himself in the foot. [9.10]

George W. Bush almost shot himself in the foot with the recurrence of the specter of the dreaded reaction shot. The television broadcasters...including Fox News, the openly pro-Bush cable channel, that provided the pool cameras for all the networks...got around the campaign committees' prohibition on such shots by using a split screen. For most of the debate, all the channels showed *both* candidates, so that, while one was speaking, the other's reactions were clearly visible.

These split screens proved to be George W. Bush's own *bete noir*. In an eerie echo of his own debate with Al Gore four years earlier, it was now the president who repeatedly expressed displeasure while his opponent was speaking. This time, it was with disdainful scowls, impatient frowns, and angry grimaces (Figure 9.6).

▲ **FIGURE 9.6** *George W. Bush scowls at John Kerry.*

In an equally eerie echo, the television cameras captured Bush's scorn, but this time, it was the Democratic party that leapt to the fore: Within 24 hours after the debate, it posted on its website a page called "Faces of Frustration," which linked to a 43-second video sequence of 14 rapidly cut shots of George W. Bush's peevish looks.*

The public reaction to the president's behavior was instant and dramatic. According to a Gallup Poll taken immediately after the debate, Kerry won by 53% to Bush's 37%. [9.11] Four days later, Gallup reported that Kerry, who had fallen behind Bush in the national preference polls since the Republican National Convention in early September, had pulled even at 49% to 49%. [9.12]

According to virtually every knowledgeable political opinion, Bush's negative behavior had damaged his own cause. One political analyst said, "The Bush Scowl is destined to take its place with the Gore Sigh and the Dean Scream." [9.13] The latter reference to Howard Dean's impassioned concession speech following his loss in the 2004 Iowa Caucuses that was widely attributed to be the cause of the subsequent failure of his candidacy. The Scowl, The Sigh, and The Scream are all counter to the biblical advice to be slow to anger.

It was the very office he was seeking to renew that tripped up George W. Bush. As the son of a president and the grandson of a senator, he managed his first term as a political aristocrat. During the 2004 campaign, a flood of books hit the market with insider accounts of the Bush Oval office. Many of them depicted him as a man living in an insulated capsule, constantly surrounded by phalanxes of protective aides who reverently called him "Sir," and rarely disagreed with him. Those who did were met with his disdain or wrath. In a way, he had been functioning as an omnipotent CEO of the nation, in much the same manner as Ross Perot had functioned in his business.

*You can see our version of this sequence on the companion DVD, available at www.powerltd.com.

Furthermore, George W. Bush had held fewer press conferences than any other president in history, thereby minimizing his exposure to tough questions from the press. Finally, all his appearances in his campaign for reelection were to pre-screened by audiences who were already ardent supporters. By the time he stepped into the arena with John Kerry, George W. Bush was a man unaccustomed to being challenged. Therefore, when Kerry took him to task in front of a huge television audience, much as Al Gore had taken Ross Perot to task, Bush, like Perot, met force with force.

For the second debate, George W. Bush turned back to agility for damage control. On October 8, 2004, he met his opponent at Washington University in St. Louis, Missouri. One of the questions was about nuclear proliferation. Senator Kerry, who answered first, was critical of the president's policies.

> *...the president is moving to the creation of our own bunker-busting nuclear weapon. It's very hard to get other countries to give up their weapons when you're busy developing a new one. I'm going to lead the world in the greatest counterproliferation effort. And if we have to get tough with Iran, believe me, we will get tough.*

When President Bush's turn came, in an attempt to lighten matters, he said:

> *That answer almost made me want to scowl. [9.14]*

President Bush turned to agility again in their third and final match on October 13, 2004, at Arizona State University in Tempe, Arizona. The moderator, Bob Schieffer of CBS, asked both candidates a question about their wives.

> *What is the most important thing you've learned from these strong women?*

George W. Bush responded:

> *To listen to them.*

The audience laughed. Then, the president used the laughter to defuse the still-lingering after-effect of his peevish performance in the first debate by adding,

To stand up straight and not scowl. [9.15]

However, that second debate in St. Louis produced yet another eerie echo of history. This time, the resonance was with Al Gore's notorious "in-your-face" move during the town hall format four years earlier. In the 2004 version of the same format, one of the citizens in the audience, Daniel Farley, asked both candidates a question about reinstituting the draft. The president answered first, and then the Senator took his turn. Mr. Kerry concluded his answer with the following words:

> *We're going to build alliances. We're not going to go unilaterally. We're not going to go alone like this president did.*

The moderator, Charles Gibson of ABC News, said:

Mr. President, let's extend for a minute...

Suddenly, George W. Bush jumped from his seat, thrust his forefinger into the air, and started striding toward Gibson, saying,

Let me just—I've got to answer this.

Gibson, trying to set up a rebuttal, said:

Exactly. And with Reservists being held on duty...

Overriding Gibson's words, Bush continued his aggressive stride. As he did, he thrust out his left arm and gestured toward Kerry.

Let me answer what he just said, about around the world.

At that moment, the television image cut to a reverse angle to show a startled Gibson (and equally startled audience members behind him) with Bush's agitated hand waving up and down in the foreground (Figure 9.7).

▲ **FIGURE 9.7** *George W. Bush approaches Charles Gibson.*

Trying to assert control of the debate, Gibson said,

> *Well, I want to get into the issue of the back-door draft...*

Overriding Gibson's words again and gathering momentum, Bush abruptly turned his back on the moderator and swung around to address the town-hall audience, his voice ringing with scorn.

> *You tell Tony Blair we're going alone. Tell Tony Blair we're going alone. Tell Silvio Berlusconi we're going alone. Tell Aleksander Kwasniewski of Poland we're going alone. There are 30 countries there. It denigrates an alliance to say we're going alone. [9.16]*

To add insult to injury, the very next night, *Saturday Night Live*, the NBC television comedy series, reinforced the incident. In its satirical version of the debate, the actor portraying Bush excitedly jumped off his stool and rudely interrupted the actor portraying Gibson.

Saturday Night Live, however, is an equal opportunity satire provider. The comedians also gave John Kerry a dose of their barbed wit. In that second debate, the senator used the phrase

"I have a plan..." 13 times, and so in that same program, the actor portraying Kerry used the phrase repeatedly, too.

However, the actual George W. Bush had only that one forceful outburst during that second engagement. The rest of the time, he contained his aggressiveness and petulance. In fact, he was a man transformed from the first debate. Every time he spoke, he did so more with animation than antagonism, and every time the reaction camera showed him listening to his opponent, George W. Bush was attentive but impassive...no frowns, no scowls.

The strategy worked. The Gallup Poll taken immediately after the second debate showed Bush did better in the match...but Kerry did better still with 47% to Bush's 45%. [9.17] Four days later, Gallup reported that Kerry still maintained a slight edge in the preference polls with 49% to Bush's 48%. [9.18]

In their third and final debate, the two candidates returned to stand up...straight this time...behind their lecterns, at a precise distance (10 feet) from each other. The separation was stipulated in the prearranged Memorandum of Understanding so that there would be no more "in-your-face" moves on each other. (Apparently, Charles Gibson was exempted as fair game.)

To further reduce the potential for conflict, the agreement also stipulated that the candidates could not question each other directly, but that did not inhibit them in the least. With this one last chance to win in the rubber match, the two men debated toe-to-toe, sharply attacking each other's policies, past performances, and even personalities. They bounced their attacks and counterattacks at each other via the moderator, Bob Schieffer, via the studio audience at Washington University, via the television audience of 51.2 million viewers, and even out into the ether.

Throughout the debate, they hurled bitter names, labels, and charges at each other with fierce intensity. Bush accused Kerry of "exaggeration," being "dangerous," making "outrageous claims," and of being "a liberal senator from Massachusetts." Kerry accused Bush of "failure," being "wrong," "misleading," a "problem," and of being "the first president in 72 years to preside over an economy in America that has lost jobs."

However, all the hostility was in their words alone. John Kerry, ever the polished debater, maintained the same calm, cool, poise and sturdy confidence he had exhibited in the first two debates. George W. Bush repeated his controlled demeanor of the second debate by being animated physically without being antagonistic. In fact, on several occasions, he added smiles to his repertory. One of them, while he was attacking his opponent's health care plan:

> *I want to remind people listening tonight that a plan is not a litany of complaints, and a plan is not to lay out programs that you can't pay for.*
>
> *He just said he wants everybody to be able to buy in to the same plan that senators and congressmen get. That costs the government $7,700 per family. If every family in America signed up, like the senator suggested, if would cost us $5 trillion over 10 years. It's an empty promise. It's called bait and switch.*

He smiled when he said "bait and switch," and then broke into a big grin when, in response to a time prompt from moderator, he added:

> *Thank you. [9.19]*

The impression that George W. Bush had made in the first debate lingered all the way through the third. A Gallup poll taken immediately after the end of the rubber match gave John Kerry another victory by 52% to Bush's 39%. [9.20]

In the next morning's edition of *The New York Times,* an analysis of all the televised debates succinctly captured and reinforced the impressions each debater made.

> *In a crucible where voters measure the self-confidence, authority, and steadiness of the candidates, Mr. Kerry delivered a consistent set of assertive, collected*

> *performances. Mr. Bush appeared in three guises: impatient, even rattled at times during the first debate, angry and aggressive in the second, [and] sunny and optimistic last night. [9.21]*

The audience perception of their widely different behaviors is clearly visible in the public opinion polls. From the very earliest moments of the 2004 campaign, armies of research organizations took the temperature of the electorate almost every day in every imaginable way. Despite slight differences in the results from the diverse organizations in one direction or another, the consensus was a dead heat. For most of that summer, each man's percentage hovered around the high 40s, unable to break into a clear majority lead. The standard polling error of plus or minus three points was rarely exceeded, in effect, confirming that the race was too close to call. Most telling were the results in Figure 9.8, redrawn from the final Gallup poll before Election Day. (Note: The results for Ralph Nader, the third-party candidate, were insignificant and therefore omitted for clarity.)

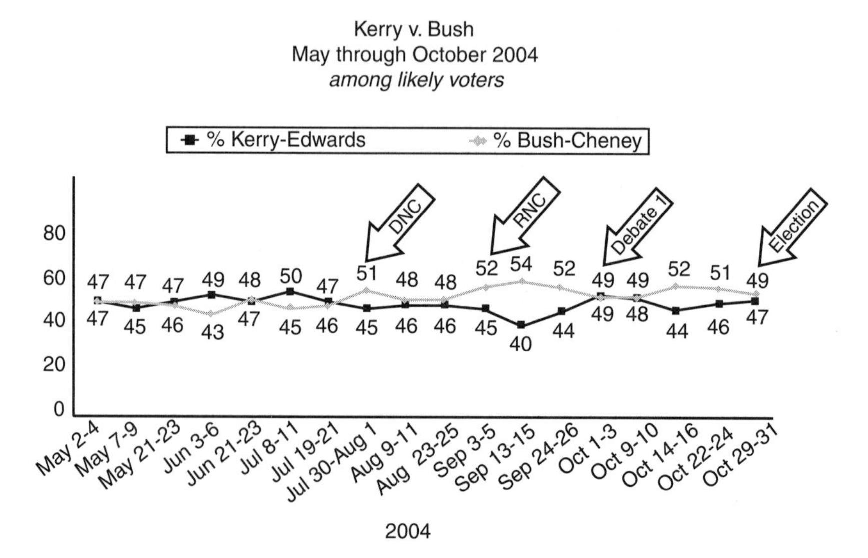

FIGURE 9.8 *Gallup Poll [9.22]*

From early May 2004, all the way through the summer, and right up to Labor Day, Bush and Kerry ran neck and neck in nearly parallel trend lines that crisscrossed like a tight pigtail. The Democratic National Convention (DNC), which took place from July 26 to the 29, in John Kerry's hometown, Boston, finally nudged Kerry just above 50%, but it was one of the smallest "bounces" any candidate *ever* got from so much media exposure. One political cartoonist lampooned Kerry's poor performance with a sketch showing a man looking at Kerry's poll results with a magnifying glass.

On the other hand, the media exposure of the Republican National Convention (RNC) in New York from August 30 to September 2 gave George W. Bush a big bounce. He surged to 54% over Kerry's 40%, a lead he held until that eventful first debate on October 3. His poor performance in that contest dropped him right back into a virtual tie with Kerry. The trend lines converged again...and then stayed very close throughout the next two debates, right up to Election Day, November 2.

In the end, however, George W. Bush won by more than 3.5 million votes. The major factor in his victory goes back to Chapter 7: his loud, clear and consistent Topspin all throughout the campaign. The president was relentless in his focus on several key messages to his key constituents, while the senator all too often shifted focus and sometimes even contradicted himself. The evidence of their differential is best seen in the election results on the national map: the blue states that went for Kerry were at the periphery of the country on the coasts and along the top, but the solid block of red states in the center...the majority...went for Bush. It was the mainstream in the heartland, responding to George W. Bush's repeated appeal to and promise of moral responsibility that awarded him his second term.

The Critical Impact of Debates

George W. Bush also succeeded in duplicating a feat that only his father, George H. Bush had accomplished...winning the election despite losing the debates. In the entire history of presidential campaigns, all the candidates (except the Bushes) who succeeded in their televised debates won their elections:

- 1960: John F. Kennedy defeated Richard Nixon in the election after he bested him in the seminal debate that set the pattern for all other debates to follow.
- 1976: Jimmy Carter defeated President Gerald Ford after the incumbent self-destructed in the second of their three debates during the Cold War when he said, "There is no Soviet domination of Eastern Europe and there never will be under a Ford administration."
- 1980: Ronald Reagan defeated Jimmy Carter after their single debate when he notably responded to Carter's position on Medicare by remarking, "There you go again!" Then, even more notably when, in his closing statement, Reagan looked into the camera and asked the nation, "Are you better off than you were four years ago?," one of the most subtle and yet powerful, and subsequently often-copied political Topspins.
- 1984: Ronald Reagan defeated Walter Mondale in a landslide after essentially breaking even in their two debates, but skewering Mondale in the second debate with his classic Topspin, "I will not make age an issue of this campaign. I am not going to exploit for political purposes my opponent's youth and inexperience."
- 1988: George H. Bush defeated Michael Dukakis in the election after losing to him in their two debates.
- 1992: Bill Clinton defeated George H. Bush and Ross Perot with his famous charisma and George H. Bush's infamous wristwatch blunder in the second of their three debates.

- 1996: Bill Clinton defeated Bob Dole with uncontested charisma not only in their two debates, but throughout the campaign.
- 2000: George W. Bush defeated Al Gore after their three debates in which he surpassed lower expectations while Gore overshot and undershot his higher expectations.
- 2004: Echoing his father's accomplishment 16 years earlier, George W. Bush defeated John F. Kerry in the election despite losing in all three of their debates. [9.23, 9.24]

Lessons Learned

The lesson here is that George W. Bush's poor performance in the first debate made a tight race out of what might have been a clear coast to victory. But the incumbent had other factors in his favor: an opponent whose frequent lapses into obscurity stood in sharp contrast to his own diligent trumpeting of his clarion call to arms, his Topspin.

The lesson for you: When you step into the line of fire, rely less on your competitor's or challenger's weakness and more on your own strengths. Take charge. Use Topspin and the many other techniques you've learned in this book to control your own destiny. In the next chapter, we'll culminate all the techniques with a positive role model from a most unlikely source, but an expert in the art of war, a military general.

> Rely on your own strengths: Take charge. Use Topspin.

The Role Model

During the 43 days of the 1991 Gulf War, General Norman Schwarzkopf, the commander-in-chief of Desert Storm, held only about half a dozen press conferences in the press room in Riyadh, Saudi Arabia, and each of those sessions was very, very brief. Despite such minimal exposure, "Stormin' Norman," as he was known, became an instant global celebrity. The reason he attracted such attention is that, in each of those sessions, broadcast live throughout the world, the general exhibited complete command and control in answering the journalists' questions. In doing so, he served as a role model for every technique you've learned...and which you would do well to emulate.

A particular case in point is the press conference of February 24, 1991. After nearly a month of air bombardments, the coalition forces launched a massive ground offensive, and General Schwarzkopf appeared to describe the first day's actions to the pool of reporters.

The general began the session by reading a brief opening statement that he concluded with the following words:

> *So far, the offensive is progressing with dramatic success. The troops are doing a great job. But I would not be honest with you if I didn't remind you that this is in the very early stages, we are a little more than twelve hours into this offensive and the war is not over yet.*

Then the general removed his eyeglasses and looked out at the sea of reporters and said,

> *That concludes my prepared comments and I am now ready to take a very few questions.*

"A very few questions." In fact, the entire Q&A session ran just two minutes and 48 seconds in real time, during which the general fielded 10 questions. The role model did what you must do in your sessions: *Manage the time.* Schwarzkopf started by setting the audience's expectations, and so must you. When you open the floor to questions, you can say that you have no time for questions or that you have all the time in the world, but set the time expectations. General Schwarzkopf did, and then he proceeded to fulfill them. He continued his time management by counting down the last few questions toward the end.

Manage the time.

But let's start with first things first...when the general opened the floor, the first reporter asked:

> *Can you give us an idea of how long, based on what you know now, if things go according to plan, how long do you anticipate this thing is going to last and how do you account for the fact that the opposition has been so light so far?*

A double question, "How long and why so light?" Two related questions. If you get multiple *un*related questions, pick only one, Buffer it, answer it, and then say, "You had another question." Because the reporter's questions were clearly related, the General fielded them both...in reverse order. The "why so light?" was first.

> *First of all I want to say that the opposition has probably been so light so far because of the excellent job that all of the forces have to date done in preparing the battlefield. With regard to your second question, it's impossible to say how long it's going to take...*

"It's impossible to say how long it's going to take," meaning that General Schwarzkopf had no intention of answering the other question about forecasting the length of the war. Instead, he said,

> *Let me put it this way. It's going to take as long as it takes for the Iraqis to get out of Kuwait and the United Nations resolutions to be enforced.*

"...the Iraqis to get out of Kuwait and United Nations resolutions to be enforced," was General Schwarzkopf's Point B, his Topspin.

If, after your business presentation, you are asked, "How long is it going to take until you release the next version of your product?" you should say, "It's impossible to say how long it's going to take." That is the Buffer using the Roman Column, *time,* as well as the candid answer. When you've done that, you can roll into your Topspin. "…but I can tell you that when the next version is released, it will have the same high quality as all the other products in our powerful pipeline and produce the same rich benefits to our customers." State your Point B and your audience's WIIFY. Seize the opportunity.

Even if you can't answer for confidential reasons, seize the opportunity to state your Point B and your audience's WIIFY.

General Schwarzkopf then recognized the next reporter, who asked:

> *There have been some reports that there has been an ongoing situation, but can you at least tell us whether we have any forces in Kuwait City? There have been reports of some paratroopers seen over Kuwait City, these reports by Kuwaiti residents.*

The Roman Column in this question was about confidential strategic information the general could not possibly broadcast to a worldwide television audience that was sure to include informants for the opposition. In business, Q&A sessions often occur at conferences where competitors are very likely to be in the audience. No businessperson or solider has any obligation to reveal strategic information and should never do so. General Schwarzkopf asserted his position. He just said, "No."

No businessperson has any obligation to reveal strategic information. Just say, "No!"

> *I'm not going to in any way discuss the location of any of the forces involved in the battle to date.*

Without missing a beat, the general then turned to another reporter who asked:

> *General have any U.S. or allied troops encountered chemical or biological weapons?*

"Chemical or biological weapons" are the key words in the question. The general rolled those key words into his answer as a Buffer.

> *We had some initial reports of chemical weapons, but those reports to date, as far as we're concerned, have been bogus. There have been no reported chemical weapons used thus far.*

Just like Colin Powell in Chapter 5, "Retake the Floor," General Schwarzkopf used the key word technique as his Buffer. And just like Colin Powell, not once during the entire Q&A session did he use a Double Buffer such as, "You'd like to know if our troops encountered any chemical or biological weapons," or a paraphrase such as, "Did our troops encounter any chemical or biological weapons?." In each of the 10 questions he fielded, General Schwarzkopf Buffered *only* with the key words and rolled them into each of his answers. Remember that the key word Buffer allows no thinking time but, when you get it right, the rapidity of your response makes you appear sharp and in control.

When you get the Key Word Buffer right, you appear sharp and in control.

The next reporter asked the General:

> *Would you say that things are going better than you expected at this stage or about on par or slightly worse?*

Better, on par, or slightly worse? A multiple choice question with three options. Which do you think the general chose? Please note that, as in earlier chapters, the rest of this page is left blank for you to think about your answer.

General Schwarzkopf chose:

> *So far we are delighted with the progress of the campaign.*

He took the opportunity to Topspin to his Point B. He took the high ground.

This next question came from a professional reporter who…as someone in your audience is very likely to do…asked a convoluted question, made more so by a halting delivery.

> *With one exception…uh… the…uh… contact with the enemy was described… you say… as light. Can you provide any details at all…*

General Schwarzkopf started to answer before the reporter even finished.

> *…about the exception?*

Before you see the general's answer, think. Specifically, what does she want to know? Please note that, as before, the rest of this page is left blank for you to think about your answer.

The reporter wanted the general to provide *details* of the *heavy* engagement. Here is his answer.

> *This afternoon about two hours ago, one of the Marine task forces was counterattacked with enemy armor. The Marines immediately brought their own artillery to bear, they also brought their anti-tank weapons to bear. We also brought our Air Forces to bear and the counterattack was very quickly repulsed and they retreated. I can't tell you the exact number or loss of tanks...*

"I can't tell you the exact number or loss of tanks." In other words, he did not give the reporter any of the details she wanted. His reply was entirely Topspin. "The Marines immediately brought their own artillery to bear; they also brought their anti-tank weapons to bear. We also brought our Air Forces to bear..." In essence, "we kicked their butts!"

> *...but there were several tanks that were lost in that particular battle.*
>
> *About two more questions.*

"About two more questions." Now he started to count down and, as he did, his answers became shorter and shorter. He also refused to take follow-on questions, which is a privilege you do not have. The next reporter asked:

> *Has the resistance been light simply because the Iraqis are retreating, or are they simply not engaging you, or are they surrendering? What exactly are they doing?*

The epitome of succinctness, General Schwarzkopf replied:

> *All of the above.*

A reporter wearing eyeglasses asked:

> *You say the opposition is light. Is this because you have avoided a frontal confrontation with them, or are you going around, or over, and is that why there is little opposition?*

General Schwarzkopf responded:

> *We will go around, over, through, on top, underneath, and any other way to get through.*

The same reporter tried a follow-on question:

> *General have you gone through sir? Is that why it's light?*

Ignoring the man with eyeglasses, the general turned to another.

> *One more.*

This journalist asked:

> *General have you encountered the Republican Guard yet?*

Moving briskly, General Schwarzkopf responded:

> *Some.*

This journalist also tried a follow-on question:

> *What kind of resistance have you gotten from that?*

General Schwarzkopf also ignored this follow-on and turned to another reporter.

> *Alright last question.*

The last question came from a man with a British accent.

> *General are you going to pursue the Iraqi soldiers into Iraq, or are you going to stop at the Kuwait/Iraq border?*

General Schwarzkopf looked straight at the man and said:

> *I am not going to answer that. We are going to pursue them in any way it takes to get them out of Kuwait.*

Then the general slapped his palm on the lectern, turned on his heel, and walked out, saying over his shoulder:

Thank you very much.

The reporter wearing eyeglasses called after him:

General, when will we see you again? Tomorrow at six? [10.1]

The general did not reply. He left his last words trailing in his wake, resonating throughout the press room, and out into millions of television sets around the globe, "We are going to pursue them in any way it takes to get them out of Kuwait," his Point B, his Topspin.

General Schwarzkopf had a number of unique control factors working for him that you and most people in business, and in most walks in life, do not share. In his press conferences, the general was the solicited party, and his audiences were the solicitors. In your Q&A sessions, the shoe will be on the other foot: You will be the solicitor, and your audiences, with whom you are trying to do business, will be the solicited. Most of the general's information fell under the cloak of tactical secrecy; most of your business information must be open and above board. The general had no need to give his media audience a single WIIFY; you have an obligation to give your audience as many WIIFYs as you can.

Nevertheless, General Schwarzkopf provided an excellent role model for all the techniques in this book:

- Manage the time
- Listen intently
- Identify the Roman Column in every question
- Buffer with the key word
- Answer succinctly
- Topspin, Topspin, Topspin

Complete Control

Figure 10.1 is a graphical representation of the dynamics of a conventional Q&A scenario. The first downward triangle in black indicates a challenging question, plunging at you like a dart to the heart. Most presenters, being results-driven, rush to provide an answer, parallel to the question, represented by the downward white triangle. These separate dynamics exert no control and add no value to the exchange.

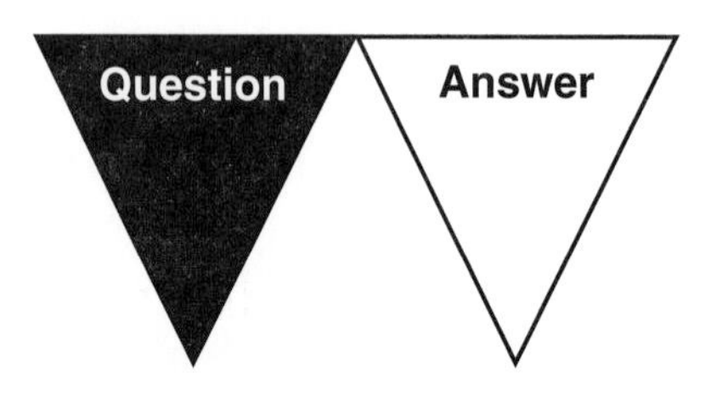

▲ **FIGURE 10.1** *Conventional Q&A dynamics.*

To assert control in your Q&A exchange, you must listen for the Roman Column during the question with the "empty cup" *concentration* of a Zen master. Then you must intervene with the two upward grey triangles in Figure 10.2.

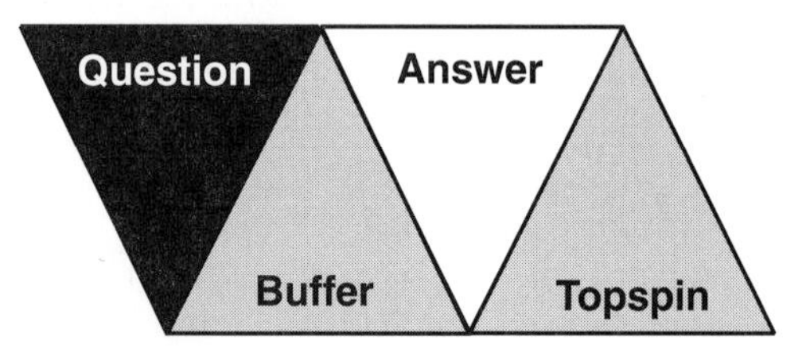

▲ **FIGURE 10.2** *Controlled Q&A dynamics.*

The first gray triangle is a Buffer composed of a paraphrase or key words to level the playing field, the equivalent of *self-defense* in the martial arts. The second gray triangle, which brackets the answer, is Topspin to your Point B and/or your audience's WIIFY, the equivalent of an *agile switch to the offensive* in the martial arts. These upward thrusts add control dynamics to the exchange.

Between the two, you must provide an answer that is the *positive Yang to balance the negative Yin* in the issue of the challenge.

When most politicians respond to questions, they jump directly to the Topspin, conveniently skipping the answer. In one of the 2000 presidential debates, then Governor George W. Bush jumped to his Topspin with an insufficient answer to Lisa Kee's question about his tax proposals. *Skipping the answer appears evasive. Never skip the answer.*

Earlier in that very same debate, however, the governor made a strong Topspin after responding to Al Gore's challenge. A little more than a year later, in a press conference at a high school in Crawford, Texas, as president, George W. Bush directly answered a question about U.S./Soviet relations and *then* added his Topspin. A little more than a year and a half after that, in his press conference on the White House lawn, he directly answered a question about his prospects for reelection and *then* moved on to his Topspin. A year after that and throughout his campaign for reelection, including all his debates, he resolutely stuck to his policy decisions in his answers and stayed on message with his Topspin.

Once you provide the answer, you can Topspin at will.

When most businesspeople respond to questions, in their eagerness to provide an effect to a cause, they jump directly to the answer, end the exchange, and then promptly move on to the next question. In the process, they bypass the opportunity to Topspin. They offer no Point B and no WIIFY. They make no call to action and give the audience no reason to act. Such behavior exerts zero control.

The winning sequence is

- Question
- Buffer
- Answer with supporting evidence
- Topspin

When you learn *all* the steps with the *discipline* of a samurai warrior and apply them with the controlled *artistry* of a symphony conductor, you combine the up and down dynamics of the triangles in Figure 10.2 and shift their direction…in *your* favor. You take complete control.

Asserting all these control techniques is no easy matter, for they require an entirely new set of skills that are counterintuitive to the reflexive Fight or Flight behavior triggered when you step into the line of fire. The challenge to achieve control is then doubled: Overcome the instincts, and learn the new skills. It is a task well worth the effort, for the outcome is also doubled: Survive and thrive *without* fighting.

P.S. The last sentence in this book is a WIIFY, my Topspin to you. Good luck!

Endnotes

Introduction

[I.1] Courtesy CNN.

[I.2] *Beowulf: A New Verse Translation* by Seamus Heaney, W.W. Norton, 2000.

Chapter 1

[1.1] *The Bob Newhart Show*, ©1975, Twentieth Century Fox Television. Written by Bruce Kane. All rights reserved.

[1.2] http://redsox.bostonherald.com/redSox/view.bg?articleid=59315.

[1.3] *Larry King Live,* Transcript, Courtesy CNN.

Chapter 3

[3.1] Debate Transcript, *The New York Times*, October 16, 1992.

[3.2] From *Newsweek* August 17, 1992 Newsweek Poll 8/6-8/7, August 31, 1992 Newsweek Poll 8/21, as published in *Newsweek* ©1992 Newsweek, Inc. All rights reserved. Reprinted by permission.

From *Newsweek* September 21, 1992 Newsweek Poll 9/10-9/11, October 5, 1992, Newsweek Poll 9/24-9/25, October 12, 1992 Newsweek Poll 10/1-2, October 26, 1992 Newsweek Poll 10/15-16, and Newsweek October 19, 1992 Newsweek Poll 10/11,

Conducted by the Gallup Organization, as published in *Newsweek* ©1992 Newsweek, Inc. All rights reserved. Reprinted by permission.

[3.3] *All's Fair: Love, War and Running for President*, by Mary Matalin and James Carville with Peter Knobler, Random House, 1994.

[3.4] http://www.debates.org/pages/trans2000c.html.

[3.5] http://www.debates.org/pages/trans2004c.html.

[3.6] http://www.debates.org/pages/trans92b2.html#q-debt.

[3.7] Carville, op cit.

[3.8] http://www.actupny.org/campaign96/rafsky-clinton.html.

[3.9] http://www.debates.org/pages/trans92b2.html#q-debt.

[3.10] *The Washington Post*, October 17, 1992.

[3.11] From *Mad As Hell* by Jack W. Germond and Jules Witcover. Copyright ©1993 by Politics Today, Inc. By permission of Warner Books, Inc.

Chapter 4

[4.1] *Zen in the Martial Arts*, by Joe Hyams, Jeremy P. Tarcher/ Perigee Books, 1979.

[4.2] From *Mad As Hell* by Jack W. Germond and Jules Witcover. Copyright ©1993 by Politics Today, Inc. By permission of Warner Books, Inc.

[4.3] http://www.debates.org/pages/trans92b2.html#q-debt.

Chapter 5

[5.1] *Secret Tactics: Lessons from the Great Masters of Martial Arts,* by Kazumi Tabata, Charles E. Tuttle Co., Inc, 2003.

[5.2] Copyright ©2000 by Houghton Mifflin Company. Reproduced by permission from the *American Heritage Dictionary of the English Language, Fourth Edition*

[5.3] http://www.state.gov/secretary/rm/2003/19662.htm.

Chapter 6

[6.1] From *The Warrior Within: The Philosophies of Bruce Lee To Better Understand the World Around You and Acieve a Rewarding Life* by John Little, published by Contemporary Books, copyright ©1996 by The McGraw-Hill Companies. The material is reproduced with permission of The McGraw-Hill Companies

[6.2] http://www.whitehouse.gov.newsreleases/2004/04/04/print/20040413-20.html.

[6.3] *The New York Times*, August 27, 2004.

[6.4] http://www.debates.org/pages/trans2004c.html.

[6.5] "Pres Hopeful Kerry Pressed On Foreign Leader Claims," Dow Jones Newswires, Wall Street Journal Online, 3/15/04.

[6.6] http://www.debates.org/pages/trans92b2.html.#q-debt.

Chapter 7

[7.1] *Secret Tactics: Lessons from the Great Masters of Martial Arts,* by Kazumi Tabata, Charles E. Tuttle Co., Inc, 2003.

[7.2] ABC News/*Nightline*, October 25, 1988.

[7.3] http://www.debates.org/pages/trans2000c.html

[7.4] http://www.whitehouse.gov/news/releases/2001/11/20011115-4. html.

[7.5] http://www.whitehouse.gov/news/releases/2003/05/20030516-15. html.

[7.6] "Election Reinforces U.S. Religious Divide," by the Associated Press, *The New York Times*, November 5, 2004. Copyright 2003 Associated Press. All rights reserved. Distributed by Valeo IP

[7.7] "Bush Drives a Wedge Through the Electorate," *Financial Times*, November 4, 2004. Reprinted by permission of Financial Times. Copyright ©2004 by The Financial Times

[7.8] http://debates.org/pages/trans88c.html.

[7.9] Debate Transcript, Courtesy CNN.

Chapter 8

[8.1] *Secret Tactics: Lessons from the Great Masters of Martial Arts,* by Kazumi Tabata, Charles E. Tuttle Co., Inc, 2003.

[8.2] *Tell Me a Story: Fifty Years and 60 Minutes in Television,* by Don Hewitt, Public Affairs 2001, 2002.

[8.3] From "Winners of the First 1960 Televised Presidential Debate Between Kennedy and Nixon," by Sidney Kraus,. *Journal of Communication*. Volume: 46. Issue: 4.Copyright ©1996 by *Journal of Communication*. Reprinted by permission of Oxford University Press.

[8.4] Transcript, Courtesy CNN.

[8.5] "An Acquired Taste," by James Fallows, *The Atlantic Monthly*, July 2000.

[8.6] *Larry King Live,* Transcript, Courtesy CNN.

[8.7] Fallows, op cit.

Chapter 9

[9.1] *The Art of War,* by Sun Tzu, Translated by Thomas Cleary, Shambala Publications, Inc., 1988.

[9.2–9.3], [9.5–9.6], [9.8], [9.10], [9.14-9.16], [9.19] http://debates.org

[9.4] http://www.cnn.com/ALLPOLITICS/

[9.7] "Gore drowns in his own honey," By Bill Press/CNN, October 12, 2000.

[9.9] http://interactive.wsj.com/edition/resources/documents/poll-20001017.html.

[9.11-9.12], [9.17-9.18], [9.20], [9.22-9.23] http://www.gallup.com/

[9.13] "Kerry looked like a leader," by E.J. Dionne, *Washington Post Writers Group*, October 2, 2004.

[9.21] "A Crucial Test, but Not Final," by Todd S. Purdum, *The New York Times*, October 14, 2004. Copyright ©2004 by The New York Times Co. Reprinted with permission

[9.24] Courtesy CNN.

Chapter 10

[10.1] ABC News video transcript.

Acknowledgments

For Power Presentations, Ltd.:

Jim Welch is technically the CPA of my company, but he is much more than that. His invaluable acumen helps me to run the business and frees me to deliver the programs that form the basis for this book. Jim is also a wise counsel in matters human and spiritual. As if all of that were not enough, Jim, who attained the Do rank of 4.0 Kyu in Shotokan Karate, validated the martial arts analogies. In fact, Jim is a Black Belt Master in life.

Nichole Nears and Jennifer Turcotte also help me operate the company, but their contributions to this book went far beyond the call of duty. Together, they performed as a research engine that out-Googled Google. Nichole also generated all the line art with the precision of an architect, tracked down the permissions with the due diligence of an attorney, managed the manuscript with the authority of a drill sergeant, and still had time to be our Web Master. Jennifer handled the source videotapes with the thoroughness of a producer and pre-screened them with the eye of a director. Surely, Ben Affleck will star her first film.

Cousin Joel Goldberg, an image-maker par excellence, lent his images and talents generously.

For the source videos:

Kenn Rabin of Fulcrum Media Services went to the ends of the earth to find and, in some cases, unearth the many video and film clip examples that support my concepts. Kenn did his searching with the patience of a monk and the knowledge of a Talmudic scholar.

Brian Fulford, the Senior Licensing Agent of CNN, provided the bulk of the source videos and was a repository of camera angles himself.

Ed Rudolph and Bob Johns, the editors who helped me grab the still frames for the book, are artists-in-residence at Video Arts, San Francisco, a superb production house managed by Kim Salyer and David Weissman. David is no relative, but I wish he were.

Rich Hall contributed mightily to the evolution of the source videos.

For the book:

Bill Immerman, my attorney, who produced the superb film, *Ray*, during the writing of this book, still found time to provide his astute counsel.

Arthur Klebanoff, a rare agent who understands ink-stained wretches because he is one himself.

Paula Sinnott, my new editor at Pearson, found new values in material that took me nearly two decades to develop.

Lori Lyons, the Pearson project editor, guided the manuscript through the complex shoals of the production process with the steady assurance of harbor pilot.

Chuck Elliot plastered many green Post-its throughout an early version of the manuscript, all of which helped me to move it to a more mature version with the blazing speed of a Curt Schilling fastball...much faster than Pedro Martinez ever could.

Quentin Hardy, whose PDA and mind are filled with valuable information from Beowulf to Burlingame and beyond.

Bruce LeBoss introduced me to the classic Bob Newhart episode.

Eric Nielsen, Senior Director, Rights and Permissions, The Gallup Organization, always exercised his attention to detail, a most suitable trait for a statistician.

Warren Drabek tracked permissions relentlessly.

For their inspiration:

Mike Wallace, Senior Correspondent for CBS *Sixty Minutes*. Heaven did help me.

Babette Cohen did not blow my cover.

Melvin Van Peebles, an entire B.E.T. unto himself, was a reality check at every step along the way, as always.

The late Kelsey Selander Phipps pointed me to the platform. The late Harry Miles Muheim, American, my first speech teacher and a superb writer, taught me to "Keep going," and became the ultimate mentor for the whole shooting match.

As a teacher on my own, I am always mindful of the Rogers and Hammerstein song from *The King and I*, in which a teacher sings of being taught by her students. Many of my student-clients have challenged me, queried me, tested me, disagreed and agreed with me, but they have all taught me to look at my own material more scrupulously and to make improvements constantly. I am particularly grateful to Vani Kola, the CEO of Certus, a company that helps other companies in the line of fire of the Sarbanes-Oxley Act. Vani's astute perceptions during her Q&A session with me added dimension to both the program and the book.

I am also grateful for the stimulating input…and continuing support…from the many people at Cisco Systems, among them Sue Bostrom, James Richardson, Peter Alexander, Toby Burton, Kaan Terzioglu, Corinne Marsolier, Mary Gorges, and Joe Ammirato; and from the many people at Microsoft Corporation, among them Jeff Raikes, Mike Nash, Kai Fu Lee, Yuval Neeman,

Pascal Martin, Vince Mendillo, Sara Williams, Ilya Bukshteyn, Dave Mendlen, Kristin Buzun, and Paul Sausville.

I am equally grateful to Microsoft alumni: Jon Bromberg, the Max Bialystock of video; Paul Gross straightened the long and winding road from Scotts Valley; Rich Tong, the champion of champions; John Zagula, who recently went through his own initiation into the literary fraternity, still found the time to give me the right sequence, the right title and, as he always does, the metaview; and Jonathan Lazarus, both a CBS and a Microsoft Emeritus and an ongoing trusted advisor, whose most memorable contribution was a Redmond-to-New York-to-Las Vegas parlay that rivaled Tinkers-to-Evers-to-Chance.

In a category all by himself is the man who bridges both the Cisco and Microsoft worlds from his lofty perch as a patron saint, Jim LeValley.

In Show Business, the closing act is reserved for the star of the show. For this Road show, that position goes to the Impresario who, with the panache of a Sol Hurok, started it all, Benji Rosen.

INDEX

A

B

C

D

E

F

G

H

I

J-K

L

M

N

O-P

Q

R

S

T

U-V

W-Z

FOR MORE INFORMATION ABOUT POWER PRESENTATIONS, PLEASE CONTACT:

Jerry Weissman
POWER PRESENTATIONS, LTD.
1065 E. Hillsdale Boulevard
Suite 410
Foster City, CA 94404-1615
650-227-1160
www.powerltd.com

In this book, you'll find many examples of Q&A sessions and political debates in the public arena. The original videos of these sessions are available on a DVD that you can obtain by visiting www.powerltd.com.

Also by Jerry Weissman

Presenting to Win: The Art of Telling Your Story

ISBN 0-13-046413-9

304 pages

$24.95 US

© 2003

Coming in paperback, 2006

Find out what Cisco, Microsoft, Intel, Intuit, Yahoo!, and many other companies have learned...that Jerry Weissman can make you a power presenter. Jerry Weissman has been a presentation coach for nearly twenty years, helping the C-level executives of America and Europe's most prestigious companies present their message to Wall Street analysts, venture capitalists, the media, and the public at large. Jerry's coaching sets his clients apart.

In *Presenting to Win: The Art of Telling Your Story,* he shows you how to connect with even the toughest audiences...and move them to action. Drawing on dozens of practical examples and real case studies, Weissman shows presenters how to identify their goals and messages; how to stay focused on what their listeners really care about; and how to capture their audiences in the all-important first 90 seconds.

Weissman covers all the practical mechanics of effective presentation, and walks readers through every step of building a Power Presentation, from brainstorming through graphics to delivery. This book's easy, step-by-step approach has been proven with billions of dollars on the line, in hundreds of IPO road shows before the world's most demanding investors.

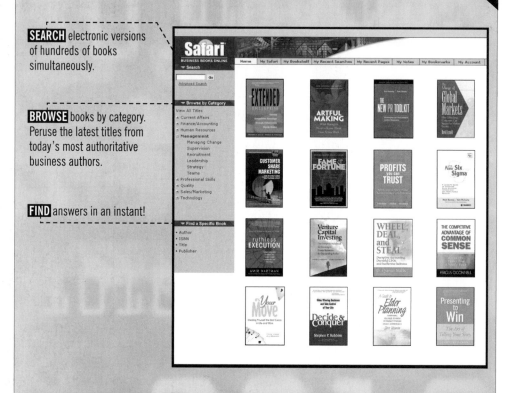